Acknowledgments

Our thanks to the Orlando Science Center and the parents and staff members at Amazing Explorers Academy in Oviedo, Florida.

Integrating Inquiry into Learning Centers

Deirdre Englehart, EdD; Debby Mitchell, EdD;
Junie Albers-Biddle, EdD; Kelly Jennings-Towle, EdD;
and Marnie Forestieri, CDA

Gryphon House
www.gryphonhouse.com

Published by Gryphon House, Inc.
P. O. Box 10, Lewisville, NC 27023
800.638.0928; 877.638.7576 (fax)
Visit us on the web at www.gryphonhouse.com.

Bulk Purchase

Gryphon House books are available for special premiums and sales promotions as well as for fund-raising use. Special editions or book excerpts also can be created to specifications. For details, call 800.638.0928.

Disclaimer

Gryphon House, Inc., cannot be held responsible for damage, mishap, or injury incurred during the use of or because of activities in this book. Appropriate and reasonable caution and adult supervision of children involved in activities and corresponding to the age and capability of each child involved are recommended at all times. Do not leave children unattended at any time. Observe safety and caution at all times.

Library of Congress Cataloging-in-Publication Data

The Cataloging-in-Publication Data is registered with the Library of Congress for 978-0-87659-402-5.

Contents

Introduction

Play has been established as a major avenue of learning for young children. Learning centers have provided opportunities for play and learning at the preschool level for years. Integrated learning centers make sense for young children because the concept aligns with the way children learn. Young children don't separate content into different areas; they naturally see and integrate learning in a holistic way as they play.

The idea of integrating science, technology, engineering, and math (STEM) into learning centers is relatively new. Although literacy integration has become more common by providing books and writing materials within learning centers, focusing on STEM in different centers is a fresh approach. Because science is an avenue for children to learn about their world, it fits naturally with learning centers. Young children's learning reflects a cycle that begins with an awareness of ideas and materials, moves to exploration with materials, then progresses as children develop concepts. This cycle of learning that occurs through explorations, inquiry, and building of knowledge uses similar processes as the engineering method and scientific inquiry. The initial explorations provide children with the experiences to build new ideas through these methods. Children need time and interactions to facilitate their learning and play. Learning centers provide a perfect platform for these experiences.

Integration of STEM in the early years exposes young children to a problem-solving approach to learning that aligns with their own curiosity. The integration of STEM in the preschool setting may spark an interest in and increase preparation in these fields in for future, which could lead to interest in STEM careers.

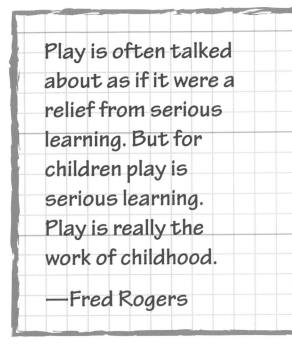

Play is often talked about as if it were a relief from serious learning. But for children play is serious learning. Play is really the work of childhood.

—Fred Rogers

How to Use This Book

Learning centers are the cornerstone of the early childhood classroom. Children love choices with the opportunity to pursue their own interests and ideas while playing in centers. Learning for young children is integrated and includes different skills and content areas. This book is designed to bring learning centers to the next level through integration of content, and to be a guide for teachers to think more broadly about children's learning options.

Each chapter focuses on a specific learning center and includes general ideas to implement various content areas within the center. These ideas can help children to extend and expand learning that naturally develops while playing with materials commonly found in the center. The second portion of each chapter focuses on a theme. This section provides ideas and activities to integrate in the learning center that are aligned with commonly used themes, such as the zoo or a restaurant.

When using this book, begin with one center, one activity, or a theme. Some lessons build on each other, but most can be used at any time to foster an integrated approach to learning. It is helpful to take time to introduce topics before children begin the center period, to interact with them during play to promote further thinking and involvement during centers, and to encourage children to share experiences at the end of centers.

Ways to Use Learning Centers

Because the goal of many of these activities is to support children's autonomy in learning centers, you may find it helpful to introduce the activities during group time, prior to releasing children to play. This format allows the teacher to reinforce specific activities that can be accomplished during centers time. Some activities will require that the teacher be more focused or involved with children at one learning center, but the overall point is to encourage children to pursue various opportunities for integrated learning during play. The following strategies can help achieve this goal.

- Whole group introduction: Select one learning center and introduce activities that are available. Teachers may find it works well to introduce one related activity for one learning center per day using the directions provided. This will help create excitement about specific learning centers and will allow the teacher to maintain a focus on that learning center for the day. The activities at specific learning centers will be available for more than one day for students who are unable to participate on the first day. The teacher also can remind students of other special activities that were previously introduced and may be ongoing in the learning centers.

- Learning center time: Release children to the learning centers. The teacher's role may be to assist, question, interact, or observe children during play. Although specific lessons are the focus, the teacher may want to dedicate more time to that learning center while still being aware of all students in the room.

- Learning review: At the close of learning centers, invite the children to come together again to discuss their learning and activities. Encourage children working on the special center lessons to share ideas related to their learning that day. Some activities in this book specifically suggest that children share their work at the end of play time.

Enjoy the activities in this book with children. Watch them during play time as they begin to think like scientists and engineers while using the tools of mathematics and technology to support their learning!

Enhancing the Focus on STEM

Current research encourages the use of play in learning for young children, and children's social development is enhanced during play interactions. Literacy research also suggests that the integration of reading and writing materials helps to support children's emergent literacy skills in an authentic way. Although our educational system recognizes the value of play in the preschool years, social development and literacy development are considered the main benefits of play for young children. Beyond these benefits, play can support children's learning in other areas, including STEM. Children's natural inquisitiveness offers early childhood teachers avenues for introducing STEM activities.

An enhanced emphasis on STEM at all levels of education is a trend gaining support. Based on the results of several national testing efforts, it is apparent that students in the United States need a stronger focus on the mathematics and science areas to be competitive globally. In early

childhood classrooms, STEM and the beginnings of STEM investigations are already happening in learning centers. Teachers can help to strengthen this type of inquiry by understanding how to integrate STEM into certain learning areas and enhance understanding through materials and interactions during play.

When you enhance the focus on STEM learning, you will allow young children to exercise their curiosity by investigating different ideas and activities during play. The learning environment should center around encouraging children to consider their questions, what they want to know, and how they can find out. You can encourage inquiry and engineering processes by talking with children about their questions and by interacting with them when they are participating in different learning centers. You can also ask questions to get children thinking. When teachers have conversations and feedback loops with young children, it can help to promote their thinking and learning processes.

When young children begin to play, they don't say, "I'm going to do science today, or maybe math. I think I'll do math today!" Instead, children think about finding out about the world around them, and the learning is all intertwined. Unconsciously, they ask questions such as, "What will happen if I move this block?" or "How far will the car go if I let it roll down this ramp?" The questions that guide children as they begin to play may not be visible unless teachers observe carefully. As teachers, our objective is to consider what children's goals are during the play and to try to support those goals.

Supporting STEM in Centers

The components of a STEM curriculum in learning centers include the following:

- Science builds on the natural curiosity of young children. In the play environment, investigations with materials lead children to discover more about their world through their everyday experiences. Encouraging children to ask questions, observe, and explain their ideas can support the development of science inquiry. Open-ended questions provide a rich context for engaging young children in meaningful conversations that can enhance their learning.

- Technology for young children includes the integration of tools that are used to support children's work. These tools can range from simple crayons, markers, and a clipboard to more sophisticated items, such as digital cameras and tablets. Many applications are available that allow young children to communicate their ideas from their learning and also support learning in content areas.

  STEM PLAY

For example, the Busy Shapes app by Edoki lets children work with matching shapes on a tablet screen and the StoryKit app lets children record themselves telling stories. Because preschoolers cannot, express themselves well through writing, these applications provide a valuable means of showing learning progress.

- The engineering process begins with a problem. Students work to consider various solutions then test out their solutions to see what works and how they can refine them. In play and learning centers, blocks and other open-ended play materials offer various opportunities for engineering activities. Children enjoy building and are often intrigued with how things work. These foundations of engineering support children's creativity as they build structures with materials during play. Providing challenges to children allows them to use their creativity and thinking skills to solve problems.

- Mathematics occurs quite naturally in play and learning centers. It can include number sense, spatial relationships, geometry, patterns, and comparisons. Math often goes hand in hand with science and engineering, as it gives children the language to share findings of investigations and problems. For example, children at the science center may investigate bones and use the mathematical concepts of measurement and comparison to explore them.

Providing Time and Materials

Providing materials along with teacher introductions and interactions during learning centers will set the stage for STEM learning. Young children need time to observe and interact with materials during play. By continually exploring with adult guidance and scaffolding, children can become better observers. You can provide a variety of materials to stimulate children's curiosity.

The learning centers should be stocked with different props and materials that will support children's learning in certain areas. The integration of STEM in various centers will allow young children to discover, explore, and work to solve problems related to each center's focus area. The teacher can further support ongoing investigations by selecting additional materials and placing them in the centers to extend children's learning.

You can use the activities in this book as a starting point to encourage children's STEM interactions with materials in play centers. As you observe children's play and developing interests, you can design other activities that guide and scaffold children's experimentation. Young children need to be able to manipulate the materials to develop their own understanding of the scientific process.

Planning for Classroom Management

Before introducing center activities, review the expectations for learning center behavior with children. The goal is to continually encourage positive patterns of behavior as children work in learning centers. Teachers can reinforce this process by reviewing instructions periodically and by having equipment organized in a manner that will promote children's ability to take things out and put them away easily and quickly. These strategies can help the learning centers run more smoothly.

Behavior Management

Teachers also can take steps to support children in their interactions with others during learning centers. If you discuss various strategies for how to take turns and collaborate during centers, children's play will go more smoothly. Occasional conflicts during play will naturally occur, as young children are still learning appropriate behaviors. By observing children's interactions in centers, you will have opportunities to step in and model strategies to use when conflict arises.

Classroom and behavior management are important elements of creating a comfortable environment for integrated learning in centers.

STEM PLAY

Art Center

The art center provides young children a place to experiment with art materials; investigate ideas; and work with various tools, processes, and media. Children's natural inquisitiveness should be encouraged as children encounter sensory experiences, learn to make choices, and communicate their ideas. Art offers enjoyment and stimulation for the imagination. Children create relationships between ideas and objects, and then link them to thoughts and actions. Opportunities to develop self-discipline, reinforce self-esteem, foster thinking skills and creativity, and practice teamwork or cooperation take place in the art center.

The art center is a place where children can develop skills across the prekindergarten curriculum. These include social-emotional skills, such as sharing materials and cooperating on projects; language and pre-literacy skills, such as describing their work and writing captions; and gross- and fine-motor skills, such as large arm movements for easel painting or cutting with child-safe scissors. Art

provides opportunities for learning in mathematics through hands-on experiences with shape, size, and measurements; in engineering through investigations of structure and function, design or composition, and three-dimensional (3-D) projects; and in science through explorations of color, shape, structure, balance, space, texture, mass, and volume.

Examples of STEM Learning

Science

- Experimenting—Asking what happens if you mix red and blue paint.
- Investigating—Looking at the different textures you can make with crayons.
- Physical science—Wondering if a clay animal will stand up on four feet.
- Problem solving—Deciding whether to use a staple or glue or tape to connect an object you're creating.

Technology

- Creativity programs—Recording your ideas using apps such as Starry Night for art and Story Kit for literature.
- Brainteaser programs—Developing your logical thinking and spatial perception by using apps such as OverColor, which challenges you to copy colorful patterns using geometric shapes.

Engineering

- Constructing—Exploring how to construct a 3-D structure of a butterfly using recycled materials.
- Designing and building—Figuring out how to make a boat out of water bottles.

Math

- Counting—Finding out how many items it will take to fill in a space.
- Geometry—Exploring what shapes you can use to make a cat.
- Measurement—Figuring out how long the line should go in a picture.
- Patterns—Creating a design with a pattern of red, blue, and green beads.

Examples in Other Areas

Literacy

- Narrative language—Describing how you used red paint and mixed it with blue to get purple.

STEM PLAY

- Oral language—Explaining how you made your colors so bright. Asking a classmate to pass the crayons.
- Written language—Labeling and writing while using invented spelling.

Social Interactions

- Cooperative play—Engaging in cooperative play with others while making items.
- Sharing—Cooperating to use materials while working together.

Physical Development

- Fine motor—Gaining practice using child-safe scissors to cut.
- Gross motor—Trying to paint with water outside along the wall using your whole arm.

Art Center Activities: No Theme

The art center is a fun area of the classroom where children can use their creativity, but the center also enhances learning in other content areas. It should be orderly and organized, and the teacher can rotate materials—such as collage items—in and out and replenish them frequently.

Using materials such as paint and glue, children can experiment with mixing colors and explore a variety of science concepts, such as different properties of liquids. The following ideas can help children extend and expand learning that naturally develops while working with materials commonly found in the center.

SHAPE PICTURES

Children will use different shapes to create their own picture.

Skills supported:

- Creating and designing
- Exploring and experimenting
- Developing fine motor skills
- Using geometry
- Developing eye-hand coordination

- Listening
- Learning about people and the environment
- Problem solving

Materials:

Attribute blocks

The Shape of Things by Dayle Ann Dodds

Construction paper

Glue

Child-safe scissors

What to do:

1. Read *The Shape of Things*.
2. Ask children to think about how they could put shapes together to make things when they are working in the art center. Ask if they could make a house like the one in the book.
3. Allow children to manipulate the shape blocks on paper to make pictures. Then encourage them to trace, cut out, and glue shapes on paper to make pictures.
4. *Alternatives:* Children can make their own shapes without tracing, or the teacher can have premade shapes cut out of construction paper.

BUILDING BRIDGES OUT OF RECYCLED MATERIALS

Use recycled materials to explore engineering concepts to build a bridge.

Skills supported:

- Creating and designing
- Exploring and experimenting
- Using creativity
- Developing fine motor skills
- Using geometry
- Problem solving
- Developing environmental awareness
- Exploring physical science (properties of matter)

Materials:

Hole punchers

Painter's tape

Pictures of bridges, such as the Golden Gate Bridge

Recycled materials, such as paper-towel rolls, cereal boxes, cardboard boxes, and paper plates

Rubber bands or twine

Scissors

What to do:

1. Tell children a story that includes a problem that could be solved with a bridge. Here is one example: "One time I was walking through the woods, and I came to a small river. I couldn't get over it because it was too wide for me to cross. So I had to walk right through the water, and it was very cold on my feet. I almost fell in the water, too."

2. Ask children questions to get them thinking about the problem: "Can you tell me the problem that I had when I was walking through the woods? What would have helped me to get over the river?"

3. Accept different answers from children. If no one suggests a bridge, add it to the ideas.

4. Show the children the pictures of bridges, and highlight the differences. You might say, "Some of the bridges are very big and long, but other ones are smaller, like one that I might need to cross the river."

5. Explain that they can visit the art center and use some of the materials there to create their own bridges.

6. Later, have children share the different ways they created their bridges.

For more support:

- Model how to make a suspension bridge.

- Cut a strip of cardboard from cereal boxes or use other cardboard to make the bridge.

- Use paper-towel rolls to make four towers (one on each corner). Cut four slits on the bottom of each roll, fold the flaps, and tape them to the ground.

- Punch holes along the sides of the bridge and make loops with rubber bands to hold twine that will act as cables.

- Connect the twine to the paper-towel rolls and experiment with how to support the weight.

TAKING SIDES

Encourage children to consider different perspectives of 3-D objects.

Skills supported:

- Analyzing
- Developing fine motor skills
- Using geometry
- Practicing inquiry
- Observing
- Noticing detail
- Developing vocabulary

Materials:

3-D objects such as dolls or stuffed animals

Paper

Crayons

What to do:

1. Begin a discussion about perspectives with children. Show them a doll or another 3-D object and ask two children to sit with one child facing the front of the object and one child facing the back. Ask the two children, "Can you tell me what you are looking at?" Discuss their answers.

2. "What do you see from your side?" Allow them to share answers.

3. Explain that when we have objects that are 3-D (not flat), we have different perspectives of how they look, depending upon which way we are looking at them.

4. Tell them that when they go to the art center, you would like for them to look at some objects and draw them from different perspectives or different angles. So, if they were looking at the doll, they might draw it from the front and the back.

5. Let them know that at the end of center time today you will ask some children to share their drawings to see if the class can guess what they drew.

TISSUE-PAPER BUTTERFLIES

Children make 3-D sculptures to learn about elements of art and engineering.

Skills supported:

- Analyzing
- Using creativity
- Developing fine motor skills
- Learning about life science
- Noticing detail
- Using patterns
- Exploring visual arts—line, shape, space, color, and texture

Materials:

Books about butterflies, such as *The Very Hungry Caterpillar* by Eric Carle

Clothespins

Markers

Other collage items, such as googly eyes, stickers, and pompoms

Pipe cleaners

Scrap paper

Tissue paper

Ziplock bags

What to do:

1. Read *The Very Hungry Caterpillar* or any other butterfly book to children.

2. Ask the children questions, such as, "What do you notice about the butterfly?"

3. Tell them that they can create their own butterflies. Ask them what parts they would like to include.

4. Let them know that the art center has materials they can use to build butterflies. Model one way to make a butterfly

for children by twisting tissue paper in the middle to make wings, using a clothespin for the body, and attaching pipe cleaners for the antennas. Or you can use ziplock bags filled with colorful tissue paper or scrap paper and then twisted in the middle and add pipe cleaners for the body and antennas.

5. Children can experiment with different ways to construct their butterflies using a variety of materials. Markers and other items can be used to decorate their butterflies.

6. Explain that once children have made their butterflies, they can leave them in the art center for other people to see!

CRACKLE PAINTING

Children learn about texture by creating crackle paintings. They look similar to raku pottery.

Skills supported:

- Using creativity
- Developing fine motor skills
- Engaging in inquiry
- Noticing detail
- Using patterns
- Exploring physical science
- Exploring visual arts

Materials:

Crayons

Photocopy paper

Paintbrushes

White glue mixed with water

Pictures or real examples of raku pottery

What to do:

1. Hold up the raku pottery or pictures. Explain that it is a special kind of pottery that has a crackled surface.

2. Pass around the pictures or have the children come up to look at the pottery. Ask them what they notice about the pottery.

3. Tell them that they can make their own crackle paintings in the art center. Explain the steps involved:

    First draw a design on a piece of paper using crayons. Make sure you color in the paper as much as you can!

Next, crumple the paper and then flatten it out.

Last, paint a coat of watered-down glue over the crayon.

Once you are finished painting, you can watch the glue fill in the spaces made by crumpling the paper.

MILK PAINTING

Children will love to see a color explosion in this simple science experiment!

Skills supported:

- Engaging in inquiry
- Developing fine motor skills
- Noticing detail
- Observing
- Exploring physical science
- Making predictions
- Exploring visual arts

Materials:

Food coloring, or liquid watercolors for more vibrant colors

Liquid dish soap

Milk

Paper—Watercolor paper or card stock

Shallow bowls, small dish with a lip, or cookie trays

Toothpicks or cotton swabs

What to do:

1. Ask the children what they think will happen if you put food coloring and soap into a tray of milk. Take comments from children.
2. Tell them that you are going to show them before they go to the art center today. Ask them to watch carefully and make observations during the demonstration.
3. To demonstrate, pour milk into a dish and add a few drops of food coloring.
4. Dip the toothpick or cotton swab in dish soap and swirl in the milk.
5. Tell the children that they can also try to do this experiment at the art center with an adult helper.
6. After they see what happens, they can each put a sheet of paper over the design to make a print.

EVERY PICTURE TELLS A STORY

Children are invited to create pictures and then tell the story that goes with them.

Skills supported:

- Using creativity
- Developing fine motor skills
- Engaging in inquiry
- Using narrative language
- Noticing detail
- Using patterns
- Exploring physical science
- Using technology
- Exploring visual arts
- Demonstrating creative expression

Materials:

Select three well-known paintings or art prints, such as *The Starry Night* by Vincent Van Gogh, *Mona Lisa* by Leonardo da Vinci, and *Boy Meets His Dog* by Norman Rockwell, and bring pictures of them

Graph with the three picture names and images

Sticky notes

Large paper

Paint

StoryKit app on an iPad, optional

What to do:

1. Introduce the activity. You might say, "Did you know . . . every picture tells a story? I have three famous pictures here. I want you to look at each one carefully. Then I will ask some people if they think they might know the story behind the picture."

2. Show the pictures one at a time, and ask for volunteers to share ideas.

3. Tell children some background information about the three photographs.

4. Ask children to think about which picture they like the best and why.

5. Tell them, "I have a graph that you can use to vote. I will call your name and you should take a sticky note and put it on the graph to show your favorite."

6. Ask children to help you count how many votes each picture has. "Count with me. Which picture has the most votes? Which picture has the least votes?"

7. Ask children to think about a picture they might want to create when they go to the art center this week. "What will you make? What story will your picture tell?"

8. If children finish their pictures in time, they may use the StoryKit app on an iPad to take pictures and record their voices telling their stories.

SYMMETRY PICTURES

Children learn about symmetry when mixing colors and folding paper.

Skills supported:

- Communicating
- Constructing
- Creating and designing
- Developing fine motor skills
- Using geometry
- Exploring spatial relations

Materials:

Seeing Symmetry by Loreen Leedy or another book about symmetry

Paper, creased in the middle

Tempera paint (red, blue, and yellow)

What to do:

1. Fold a variety of square and rectangle sheets of paper in half to make a crease and leave them in the center.

2. Explain that when something is symmetrical, it is the same on both sides.

3. Tell children you have a story you can read called *Seeing Symmetry* by Loreen Leedy (or another book title).

4. After finishing the story, ask children to think about symmetry and discuss it. "What can you tell me about symmetry? What is something that is symmetrical?"

5. Tell children that in the art center they will be able to experiment with pieces of paper and different colors to make their own symmetrical pictures.

6. Ask them to drop a few different colors on one side of the paper near the crease. Then they can fold the paper on the creased line and press down to discover how the colors appear in a symmetrical pattern.

7. Ask children to tell another child about their picture or write about it once the paper dries.

Art Center Activities Using the Theme of Color

This section focuses on using color as a theme in the art center. Themes can be engaging for young children and can help focus various activities around a specific topic.

Use the engineering method for each integrated unit and lesson, as follows:

Ask: Define the problem and the research needed.

Imagine: Problem solve and be creative.

Plan: Think about what might work.

Investigate: Craft your creation and test it.

Communicate: Discuss your creation and redesign it.

Have the children keep all of their work products from the color activities so that you can collect them into a class color museum at the end of your work with the theme.

SCIENCE-INQUIRY AND ENGINEERING-METHOD CHALLENGE WITH ART

The science-inquiry and engineering-method challenge can be used at any time in the art center. It is designed to propose a problem for children that will require them to use critical thinking, planning, and inquiry to solve. The challenge is: Can you create your own colored animal and find a place for him to hide outside the classroom?

Skills supported:

- Analyzing
- Constructing
- Creating and designing
- Developing fine motor skills
- Using creativity
- Problem solving
- Exploring visual arts

Materials:

The book *A Color of His Own* by Leo Lionni

Glue, string, and other art materials

Paint

Recycled materials

What to do:

1. Read the book *A Color of His Own* by Leo Lionni to the children. The story introduces a lot of different animals, but the chameleon is trying to find a color of his own.

2. Explain the problem to the class, using the engineering method.

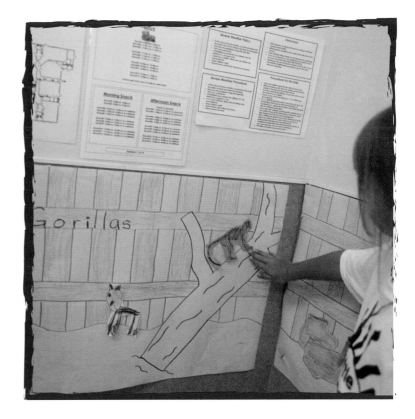

Problem: Can you create your own colored animal and hide him outside?

Ask: How could you create a chameleon or other creature? What materials will you need?

Imagine: Imagine where your creature would hide outside.

Plan: Make a plan to create your creature.

Investigate: Make your creature and paint him a color so that he would blend in. Put your creature outside to see if his color works.

Communicate: Discuss what you did and decide if you need to make any changes.

COLOR OF THE DAY

Throughout the color theme, you can designate a color of the day in the art center. Include items only of that color for children to explore. For example, on blue day, pull out blue construction paper, blue ribbons, blue paint, blue markers, blue crayons, blue yarn, and so on. Start with the primary colors of red, blue, and yellow. Then move to secondary colors such as orange, green, and purple. (Include the two primary paint colors that make up each secondary color.)

Skills supported:

- Analyzing
- Creating and designing
- Developing fine motor skills

- Exploring visual arts
- Developing vocabulary
- Developing social-emotional skills

Materials:

Collage items

Construction paper

Crayons

Glue, tape, or stapler

Markers

Old magazines

Paint

Child-safe scissors

What to do:

1. Explain to the children that during the next few days when they visit the art center, they can make special pictures called collages. Each day the class will focus on one color for the collage. Children might want to go to the art center when their favorite color is available.

2. Tell children you will look at the color words together. Explain that you will hold up a card with the color word and color, and you would like for them to help you say the word.

3. Encourage children to make collages by gluing or attaching items and pictures cut from magazines for the color of the day.

4. At the end of centers, allow children to share their artwork with others.

COLOR WALK

This activity will encourage children to notice the colors around them as they take an observation walk to look for colors.

Skills supported:

- Communicating
- Demonstrating creative expression
- Using emergent writing
- Observing
- Learning about people and the environment
- Exploring visual arts

Materials:

Clipboards

Colored pencils or crayons

Paper

Pencils

What to do:

1. Explain that today, before they go to learning centers, children will take a walk around the classroom to look for certain colors. If they see something that is blue (or another color you ask them to look for), they can draw a picture of it on paper and write about it.

2. At the end of the walk, ask, "Who can tell me something that they saw that was the color blue? How about green? Yellow?"

3. Tell children that when they visit the art center, they can draw and write about the colors they see.

MIXING PRIMARY COLORS

Children will enjoy watching two primary colors mix together to create the secondary colors of orange, green, and purple.

Red + yellow = orange
Yellow + blue = green
Red + blue = purple (violet)

Skills supported:

- Constructing
- Creating and designing
- Exploring and experimenting
- Developing fine motor skills
- Observing
- Exploring physical science
- Developing social-emotional skills
- Exploring visual arts

Materials:

The book *Mouse Paint* by Ellen Stoll Walsh

Liquid watercolor or food coloring and water in red, blue, and yellow

Ice cube trays or egg cartons

Medicine droppers

Paper for painting

Paper towels or coffee filters

Tempera paint in red, blue, and yellow

What to do:

1. Read *Mouse Paint* by Ellen Stoll Walsh to the class. Ask children, "What happens in the story with the three jars of paint—red, blue, and yellow?"

2. Explain that at the art center, they can find paint or colored water to create secondary colors. They can combine red and blue, yellow and blue, and red and yellow.

3. Tell them that they can experiment with the paint colors to make new colors.

4. For tempera paint, have containers of red, blue, and yellow paint for children to combine and make secondary colors.

5. Children can mix two colors at a time by painting one color on top of the other. Or they can pour small amounts of paint into different sections of an egg carton or ice cube trays and mix to make different colors. Then they can use the colors to paint on paper.

6. For colored water, have jars of red, blue, and yellow water for children to combine two colors at a time using a medicine dropper. They can mix colors in different sections of an egg carton or ice cube trays, and then paint on paper. Or they can drop two different colors on paper towels or coffee filters to make secondary colors.

7. Ask children to try painting on different textures and observe how the colors expand on the different types of paper.

LITTLE BLUE AND LITTLE YELLOW

Read about friendship and the combination of yellow and blue to make green.

Skills supported:

- Communicating
- Constructing

- Creating and designing
- Developing fine motor skills
- Exploring physical science
- Developing social-emotional skills
- Exploring visual arts

Materials:

The book *Little Blue and Little Yellow* by Leo Lionni

3 bowls

Spoons

Cookies

White frosting

Yellow and blue food coloring

What to do:

1. Read the story *Little Blue and Little Yellow* by Leo Lionni to the children before going to learning centers.

2. Get them thinking by asking questions such as, "What adventures did Little Blue and Little Yellow have? What happened when they hugged each other?"

3. Explain that they can retell the story of Little Blue and Little Yellow in the art center! One person can mix yellow food coloring in a bowl with white icing and one person can mix blue food coloring into a different bowl with white icing.

4. Next, each child will put both colors on a cookie and mix them together to make green frosting.

5. After icing their cookies, children can tell their classmates what their favorite part of the story was!

PAPER-TOWEL ART

This activity is a fun way for children to learn about water absorption.

Skills supported:

- Communicating
- Constructing
- Creating and designing
- Developing fine motor skills
- Exploring physical science
- Developing social-emotional skills
- Exploring visual arts

Materials:

Cookie sheets (or plastic trays)

Paintbrushes or medicine droppers

Paper towels

Washable markers

Water

Twist ties or pipe cleaners

Glue

Googly eyes, bendy straws, and other decorations

What to do:

1. Tell the children that they can do a new experiment in the art center.

2. Explain that first they will scribble with markers on a paper towel. "Scribble as much as you can!"

3. Second, they will put the paper towel on a cookie sheet.

4. Third, they will use the medicine dropper or a paintbrush to wet it.

5. Ask children, "Who can tell me what to do first, second, and third?" Allow children to explain the steps.

6. Tell them that after they do all three steps, they should watch what happens!

7. Let them know that after their paper towels dry, they can make them look like butterflies or flowers by gathering the middle part of the paper with a pipe cleaner. Demonstrate this for children.

8. Children then can decorate their butterflies or flowers with assorted materials such as googly eyes and bendy straws.

COLOR WHEEL

Children will learn about primary and secondary colors by mixing colors and making a color wheel of six colors. This activity gives children opportunities to work together in groups.

Primary colors: red, yellow, and blue
Secondary colors: orange, green, and purple (violet)
Intermediate colors: yellow-green, blue-green, blue-violet, red-violet, red-orange, and yellow-orange

Skills supported:

- Constructing

- Creating and designing

- Developing fine motor skills

- Exploring physical science
- Developing social-emotional skills
- Exploring spatial relations
- Practicing teamwork
- Exploring visual arts

Materials:

Example of color wheel

Paper plates

Child-safe scissors

Tempera paint in red, blue, and yellow

Paintbrushes

Black marker

What to do:

1. Let children know that they can work in groups in the art center to make color wheels. Show children an example of a color wheel with primary and secondary colors.

2. Ask children if they know which colors they need to mix to get each of these secondary colors. Discuss primary and secondary colors and review what children know.

3. Ask children to work in a group of six, so each can have the job of painting one of the primary or secondary colors on a plate. They will eventually cut their plate into six sections and share their colored sections so each person in the group can make their own color wheel.

4. Let three children paint a paper plate with one of the primary colors (red, blue, or yellow), and let the other three mix two primary colors to paint a plate in one of the secondary colors (purple, green, or orange). Make sure you have each color assigned to one child in a group of six.

5. Let the children know that you will have to wait for the plates to dry, and they might have to come back to the project the next day.

6. Once the paper plates are dry, use a black marker to draw lines dividing each plate into sixths. Each child can cut up her plate, or you can cut the plates into sixths yourself.

7. Each child can then take one of each color—red, blue, yellow, purple, green, and orange—and glue them in order on a clean paper plate. Provide support, such as, "Make sure you put the sections in order. Which color goes between red and blue? Which color goes between red and yellow?"

THE COLOR OF MUSIC

This activity will help children connect different feelings expressed in music to different colors.

Skills supported:

- Communicating
- Practicing creative movement
- Developing social-emotional skills
- Listening to music
- Developing cultural appreciation and understanding
- Expressing emotions
- Developing fine motor skills
- Exploring visual arts

Materials:

The book *My Many Colored Days* by Dr. Seuss

Device that plays audio recordings

Music recordings from many different cultures

Paint

Paper

What to do:

1. Before going to learning centers, read *My Many Colored Days* by Dr. Seuss to children.

2. Ask children, "What color tells how you feel today?"

3. Help them get started by describing how music makes you feel. You might say, "Sometimes when I listen to music, I feel different ways. Some music is fast, some is slow, some can be loud and some can be soft."

4. Explain that when they visit the art center, they can turn on a recording of music to listen to as they paint. Prompt them to express their feelings by saying something like, "As you listen to the music, try to think of how the music makes you feel and the colors that go with the music."

THE COLOR OF MY FOOD

Children will use plastic food from the dramatic play center to sort. They will then create 3-D objects and categorize them into colors.

Skills supported:

- Communicating
- Creating and designing
- Developing fine motor skills
- Sorting

Materials:

Air-dry clay pieces in plastic bags

Colored food from the dramatic play area

Paint

Paper napkins

Paper plates

Sorting tray

What to do:

1. Gather the children together before sending them to learning centers. Tell them that you are putting some plastic food into the art center for them and that they can organize and sort the food by colors.

2. Show the children the fruits and vegetables. Ask them if they can think of other fruits and vegetables that are different colors.

3. Explain that after they sort the foods by colors, they can create their own 3-D fruit or vegetable using the air-dry clay. Ask children to select one piece of clay each to use and shape it to look like a fruit or vegetable.

4. After they finish, they can put their creations on paper plates with their names on them. Explain that later in the week after the objects dry, they can paint their fruits and vegetables.

RAINBOW CONNECTION

Children will use a prism and flashlight to create a rainbow. They will observe the colors of the rainbow!

Skills supported:

- Using emergent writing
- Engaging in inquiry
- Noticing detail
- Observing

Materials:

Chart paper

Marker

Flashlight

Glass of water

Prism

Window with light

What to do:

1. Create a small chart with the following question at the top: "Have you ever seen a rainbow?" Under the question, make two columns, with *Yes* and *No* as headings. Post the chart, and invite each child to write her name in one column to indicate her experience.

2. Follow up with discussion questions such as, "What is a rainbow? When do you see one?" Encourage children to share and discuss their ideas.

3. Explain that a rainbow in nature is caused when the sun's light shines through drops of water during or after the rain. Ask children if they think we could make our own rainbow in the classroom. Take suggestions from children.

4. If there is a window with light shining into the classroom, place a glass of water on the window sill where it catches the light. Put white pieces of paper on the floor where the light shines to show the rainbow. You may need to adjust the positioning of objects to get a rainbow.

5. Let children know that when they go to the art center, they will see a prism and flashlight. Ask them to experiment with making their own rainbows appear. They can also create their own rainbows on paper.

6. After learning centers are complete, ask children if they can name the colors in a rainbow.

7. Ask if they think they could take a photo of a rainbow and have it show up.

8. If desired, experiment with taking photos of rainbows and letting the children see what appears in the photo.

THE COLOR MUSEUM—CULMINATING ACTIVITY

Children will take all of the work they created as a part of the color theme and create a class book and museum for other classes to visit.

Skills supported:

- Communicating
- Learning about people and the environment
- Using technology
- Problem solving

Materials:

All of the items children created from the color unit

Paper

Pencils

Crayons

Camera, iPad, or tablet computer with camera

What to do:

1. Remind children that you have been working with different colors. Ask questions to revisit their learning. "Can anyone tell me how to make the color green? What about orange?"

2. Let them know that today you will begin organizing your color museum. Explain that a museum is a place where you display different art or materials that people have created or found. Tell them that as they create the museum, you would like for them to take pictures and record what they know about colors. Explain that they can use the camera (on the iPad or tablet, or a stand-alone camera) to take pictures of their work and record what they know about colors by using the audio or video recording features. Show the children how to do this by modeling. If these tasks are beyond their capabilities, help them photograph and record. Another option is for children to draw pictures of what they made.

3. Explain that once they have shared information on colors, they can begin to organize what they created so that other classes are able to visit and see the class museum. Ask, "How can we share what we did with other classes?" Take ideas from children, and help them organize the art center and other areas if necessary.

3

Block Center

We all know that block play helps children build many different kinds of skills, including gross and fine motor development, exploring spatial relationships, thinking critically, learning to work together, and more. But let's think about the block center as a space for integrated learning.

What, exactly, is *integrated learning*? It is the way children learn naturally, as their learning overlaps different content and developmental areas.

Using the open-ended learning-center approach to integrate learning provides so many great opportunities for children to explore and learn! The block center—that staple of preschool classrooms—is a place where children can develop skills across the pre-K curriculum, including social-emotional skills, such as cooperating and waiting for a turn; language and preliteracy skills, such as creating street signs and labeling structures; and fine motor skills. Blocks also provide opportunities for learning in mathematics through hands-on experiences with shape,

size, and measurement; in engineering through investigations of structure and function; in science with explorations of structure, balance, space, and gravity; and in early literacy by using them with materials such as books, clipboards, and writing supplies.

Examples of STEM Learning

Science

- Comparison—Examining if your building is large enough for a toy car.

- Experimenting—Wondering if the castle will stand when you roll a ball against it, then finding out.

- Problem solving—Figuring out how to make a road to get the toy trucks to the store that your classmate has built.

- Physical science—Examining if a bridge will stay up if you build it across two towers.

Technology

- Programs for building—Practicing how you can move, stack, and line up parts to build structures.

- Devices—Recording your ideas by taking photos and videos, and making audio recordings.

Engineering

- Building—Creating a racetrack for the toy vehicles.

- Designing—Planning how to build a home for a toy giraffe.

- Constructing—Exploring construction with simple machines, such as ramps and levers.

Math

- Counting—Figuring out how many blocks long your racetrack is.

- Geometry—Building your whole house out of triangle-shaped bricks and noticing that triangles have three sides.

- Measurement—Determining that your building is four hands tall.

Examples in Other Areas

Literacy

- Emergent writing—Using invented spelling to label and write.
- Narrative language—Describing what you are doing: "I made a house and these people are driving around."
- Oral language—Asking questions: "What are you building? Can I build with you?"

Social Interactions

- Cooperative play—Playing in a respectful way and sharing with others.
- Sharing—Working and playing cooperatively and sharing materials.

Physical Development

- Fine motor—Using coordination to manipulate blocks in structures.
- Gross motor—Moving, sorting, and arranging larger blocks.

Block Center Activities: No Theme

The block center can enhance options for exploring various content areas. This center encourages children to use their natural inclinations for building and creating things. The ideas in this section encourage children to move beyond typical activities using blocks and link to several content areas.

WHAT I CAN BUILD

This is a great activity to use at the beginning of the year, when you are introducing the learning centers to the children. Talk with the children about your expectations for the block center—share, do not throw blocks, put your blocks away when you are finished, and so on—then brainstorm with them about the kinds of structures they could build in the center.

Skills supported:

- Using emergent writing
- Developing fine motor skills
- Listening
- Developing social-emotional skills
- Developing vocabulary

Materials:

Chart paper

Child-safe scissors

Glue sticks

Marker

Old magazines

What to do:

1. Gather the children and talk about the block center. Talk about what kinds of materials they will find there, and discuss your expectations for their behavior when they are in that center.

2. On a large piece of paper, write, "What I Can Build." Read the words to the children, then ask them to tell you their ideas for structures they could build. Record their ideas on the chart. For example, they might say a castle, horse corral, tower, bridge, office building, road, or zoo.

3. Give the children the old magazines and child-safe scissors, and ask them to find and cut out photos to show what the words represent. For example, for a horse corral, they might find a photo of a horse; for a castle, they might find photos of a crown and a real castle.

4. Let the children help you glue the pictures onto the chart next to the words they represent.

5. Read the words again with the children, and point to each picture to help them recognize and remember what the words are.

6. Tell the children that you will post the chart in the block center. When they need ideas for structures they can build, they can look at the chart.

OUR BOOK OF BUILDINGS

Children are often reluctant to put the blocks away when they have worked so hard to build their structures. This activity is a great way to help children record and remember what they have created—and to inspire their future creations!

Skills supported:

- Demonstrating creative expression
- Developing fine motor skills
- Using narrative language
- Developing print awareness
- Using oral language
- Developing social-emotional skills
- Using technology

Materials:

Blocks

Camera (optional)

iPad (optional)

Markers or crayons

Paper

Story-creation app such as StoryKit for iPad (optional)

What to do:

1. When the children are building structures in the block area, talk with them about what they are building.

2. When a child has completed a structure, encourage him to create a drawing or take photos of his building.

3. If you have a camera and software available, help the child record his structure and tell about it using a story-creation app such as StoryKit. As more children create and photograph structures, they can add to the class collection, creating a class book of building ideas. Print out pictures of the structures or the stories created on StoryKit and have them in the block center for children to review.

4. If the child has drawn a picture on paper, let him dictate to you what he wants to say about his structure; copy his story word-for-word on the back of the paper or on a separate sheet of paper. Add his drawing and story to the class book of building ideas. Keep the book in the block center for the children to look at whenever they wish.

BLUEPRINTS

Blueprints are diagrams that tell architects, engineers, and builders how to construct a building. The children can create their own blueprints to help them record all their great ideas and remember how to do them again.

Skills supported:

- Communicating
- Comparing items

- Developing visual or physical models
- Developing fine motor skills
- Noticing details
- Developing vocabulary

Materials:

Blocks

Blueprints of different structures (optional)

Dark blue construction paper

White crayons

What to do:

1. Ahead of time, build a small structure with the blocks on top of a sheet of blue construction paper.

2. Gather the children and invite them to talk about buildings. Ask them, "How does someone build a house? How does a builder know what to do?"

3. Talk with them about how builders and architects use designs called blueprints to show them what to do. If possible, show them a real blueprint. If you do not have a real one, you can find photos of blueprints on the Internet. Point out that the blueprint shows an outline of the outside of the structure and lines to show the walls, rooms, and doors inside it.

4. Show the children the structure you built earlier. Tell them that you want to make a blueprint of the building design so you can build it again later. Using a white crayon, carefully trace around the outside of the structure. Then, remove a few blocks at a time and fill in the inside of the blueprint with lines to indicate where walls and doors should go.

5. Hold up the blueprint and show the children the parts of the design. Tell the students that you have included materials in the block center for them to use to make their own blueprints.

6. As the children create blueprints, collect the designs in a class book that they can use again and again.

A BLUEPRINT HELPS ME BUILD

When the children have created a collection of blueprints, they can use them to try rebuilding their classmates' creations.

Skills supported:

- Comparing items
- Counting
- Developing visual or physical models

- Developing fine motor skills
- Measuring
- Noticing details

Materials:

Blocks

Clipboards

Collection of child-made blueprints

Pencils or crayons

What to do:

1. Remind the children that blueprints are like picture directions—they are designs of buildings. They help a builder, engineer, or architect know how to build a structure. Remind them that the class has a whole book of blueprints of children's designs. Ask the children how they could copy someone else's building. If Jana builds a great structure with blocks, how would someone else be able to build one just like it?

2. Select a blueprint, and show the children that the design shows how to build the structure. Build the structure with the blocks.

3. Let the children use the blueprints in the block center to rebuild their favorite structures.

CUBIST ART

Cubism is a style of art in which the artist incorporates geometric shapes into the work. Children can become familiar with different shapes by combining blocks in different ways. In this lesson, children can begin to look for shapes in various pieces of artwork and create cubist artwork.

Skills supported:

- Comparing items
- Counting
- Developing visual or physical models
- Developing fine motor skills
- Using geometry

- Measuring
- Noticing details
- Observing

Materials:

Various pictures or copies of artwork showing cubism

Blocks

Brushes

Easels or clipboards

Paint

Paper towels

Shape-word-and-picture cards

Water

Waxed-string sticks or similar craft tools

What to do:

1. Ahead of time, hang pictures of cubist style works of art, which incorporate geometric shapes.

2. Gather children and ask them to look at the artwork and make observations. Ask them questions to prompt close observation, such as, "What do you see? Do you see any shapes? Who can find a square shape in a picture? Who can find a circle shape? Who can find a rectangle shape in a picture? How does this artwork make you feel?"

3. Invite children to use waxed-string sticks or similar craft tools to trace the shapes on the pictures.

4. Let the children find the shape-word-and-picture cards to show the shapes they found.

5. Invite the class to say the shape words with you.

6. Give the children different building blocks and the waxed-string sticks. Encourage them to create pictures by putting different-shaped blocks onto the paper and placing the sticks around the blocks to make shapes on the paper.

7. Invite children to use paints and other art supplies to complete their cubist art pictures.

8. Display student work in the block center.

BUILDING CHALLENGE CARDS

Children love to build and create with blocks. With many experiences, children will naturally progress to more difficult structures. The design cards used in this activity can expand children's building ideas and provide a fun challenge in the building area.

Skills supported:

- Developing visual or physical models
- Developing fine motor skills
- Exploring physical science
- Exploring spatial relations

Materials:

Blocks

Paper or pencils

Premade cards that show the outline of structures that can be built with blocks

Timer (optional)

What to do:

1. When children are building in the block area, remind them about what they did with blueprints and ask them to recall the purpose of blueprints. Explain that this time they will use a different design model called *building challenge cards* (see examples below of structures that could be pictured on the cards). Ask children to tell you what a challenge is. Explain that a challenge is something new and different that they might not have done before and that it might take them a few tries before they can do it.

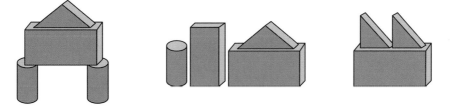

2. Ask the children to help you complete one challenge card. As you show the card, ask them what blocks are needed to build this challenge.
3. Demonstrate how to look at the card and then build a structure that follows the design on the card.
4. Tell the children that you will add the challenge cards to the block center so they can try some new challenges.

DREAMING UP BUILDINGS

Children's books can inspire ideas for building and motivate children to pursue different types of structures.

Skills supported:

- Communicating
- Exploring emergent reading skills

- Developing fine motor skills
- Listening
- Noticing details

Materials:

A variety of blocks and other building materials

Dreaming Up! by Christy Hall

Chart from What I Can Build activity

Markers

What to do:

1. Ask children to look at the What I Can Build chart. Note that you have some great builders in the classroom, and they have already created lots of great structures.

2. Explain that you will read the *Dreaming Up!* book, which shows some great buildings. Tell children that the book might give them ideas for new things they can build.

3. After reading the story, you might ask, "What building did you like from the book? Can you create something like that in the block center?"

4. Invite children to share with you what they want to build from the story. Tell children that you will leave the book in the block center for them to review.

5. Provide other books about buildings and structures in the block center:

    Arches to ZigZags by Michael Crosbie

    Shape Capers by Cathryn Falwell

    This Is Our House by Michael Rosen

    Tools by Ann Morris

CHANGES, CHANGES

Children love to tell stories. The book *Changes, Changes* tells a story with blocks. In this activity, children are challenged to tell the story from looking at the pictures in the book. They can also think of their own story while building.

Skills supported:

- Demonstrating creative expression
- Listening
- Using narrative language
- Noticing details
- Using technology

Materials:

Blocks

Changes, Changes by Pat Hutchins

Camera, iPad, or tablet computer with camera and microphone

Story-creation app such as StoryKit (optional)

What to do:

1. Gather the children and introduce the book *Changes, Changes.* Tell children that the story you are reading today does not have any words, so you need for them to help tell the story. You might say, "In most picture books, we read words and look at pictures. The words and pictures together tell the story. Because this book has only pictures, we will add words to the story."

2. Invite children to look at each picture spread in the book. After looking at the pictures, call on a child to tell the story based on the picture. Continue this way until you have finished reading the book.

3. Ask children if they can make a block structure that is similar to something in the book. Ask them to think about what stories they can tell with their blocks.

4. Help children take pictures of the structures and record the words of their stories using a story-creation app, such as StoryKit.

THE CLASS BLOCKS ROCK!

Children love to see themselves in pictures. For this activity, the whole class will have their individual class photographs and names taped to unit blocks along with pictures and names of school objects to use during their block play.

Skills supported:

- Comparing items
- Using creativity
- Exploring emergent reading skills
- Displaying self-confidence
- Developing vocabulary

Materials:

Unit blocks

Tape

Small, printed photographs of each child

Small, printed photographs of school objects (such as a desk, chair, computer, slide, swing, and flag)

What to do:

1. Ahead of time, take individual pictures of each child and various classroom objects.

2. Print them out on paper in a size that will fit on unit blocks, and write the child's or object's name underneath the image. Tape the labeled images to unit blocks.

3. Gather children around. Ask them to look at the pictures and blocks. Ask what they see.

4. Invite children to raise their hands if they can find the block with their picture on it. Ask what other pictures they recognize on the blocks. Note that the blocks have a picture of everyone in the class. They also have pictures of other things you might find at school. Ask children to help you read the words together. Tell them, "We will look at the pictures and say each word slowly. I will help you read them."

5. Explain that when they are building in the block center, they can use any of these special blocks with pictures to create a school of their own.

I'VE BEEN WORKING ON MY BUILDINGS

Children love music, and this catchy song can be sung as they work and play in the block center!

Skills supported:

- Demonstrating creative expression
- Exploring emergent reading skills
- Practicing creative movement
- Listening to and singing music

Materials:

Song lyrics for "I've Been Working on the Railroad" and audio recording (optional)

Device for playing audio recording (optional)

Chart paper

Marker

Drawing paper

Crayons or colored pencils

Tape

What to do:

1. Tell children that when you were growing up, you learned a song about building railroads. You might say, "A long time ago, when men used to work on the railroad and build railroad tracks, they would sing to pass the time."

2. Explain that today they will learn a song that they can sing while they work on their buildings in the block center. Tell them that you will sing it once and then the children can join in. Note that you will point to the words as the class sings together. Read the words of the song that follows, pointing to each word to help children recognize and remember the words.

    I've been working on my buildings, all the livelong day.

    I've been working on my buildings, just to pass the time away.

    Can't you see what I've been building, made of blocks, not straw or hay?

    Can't you see what I've been building, all the livelong day?

3. Tell children that if they would like, they can draw pictures of the buildings they want to create in the block center.

4. If an iPad or tablet computer is available, you can use one of these devices to record children singing the song.

5. Afterward, you can tape their pictures on the chart paper with the song lyrics.

6. Ask children to sing the song again along with the recording as you point to the lyrics.

ENGINEERING-METHOD CHALLENGE WITH BLOCKS

You can challenge children at any time to use scientific inquiry and the engineering method in the block center. You will propose a problem for children that will require critical thinking, planning, and inquiry to solve. The challenge for the block center is: Can you build a bridge for the three Billy Goats Gruff out of blocks?

Skills supported:

- Communicating
- Creating and designing
- Exploring and experimenting
- Developing fine motor skills
- Engaging in inquiry
- Listening
- Measuring
- Noticing details

Materials:

Models of goats

Chart paper

Different types of blocks

Markers

Measuring tape

The story "The Three Billy Goats Gruff"

What to do:

1. Read the story "The Three Billy Goats Gruff." Ask children to retell the story.

2. Pose the challenge for children, saying something like, "I heard the Billy Goats Gruff had a problem. They can no longer use the troll bridge to cross the river to get to the other side, and they need help. Can you build a bridge that would allow the Billy Goats Gruff to get to the hillside to make themselves fat?"

3. Remind children that they can use the engineering method to work on this challenge.

    Problem: Build a bridge for the Three Billy Goats Gruff that will cross a river 8 inches wide.

    Ask: How can you build a bridge for the three Billy Goats Gruff?

    Imagine: Begin to list all possible ideas of how to create a bridge that would meet the criteria.

Plan: Decide how you can build and test the bridge. What materials do you need?

Investigate: Build your bridge and test it to see if it works. Take photos or draw the results.

Communicate: Share what you learned and how you might make the bridge better.

4. Ask children to share ideas for building a bridge for the three Billy Goats Gruff. Record ideas for children on chart paper.

5. The bridge for the Billy Goats Gruff would need to cross a river that is 8 inches wide. Use the ruler to show children 8 inches. Ask children if they can build a bridge and then measure the bridge with the ruler to see if it is wide enough to cross the river.

6. Demonstrate how to make a simple bridge by using tall thin blocks for piles and a larger long block for the beam or deck of the bridge.

7. Give children blocks and let them explore creating bridge designs.

8. Invite children to tell about their designs.

Block Center Activities Using the Zoo Theme

In this section you will find activities that allow you to integrate the zoo theme into the block center. Throughout all the zoo-related activities, children will work on the overall engineering problem of building a zoo.

Problem: Build a zoo.

Ask: How can you build a zoo for some animals?

Imagine: Decide what animals should be in the zoo.

Plan: Determine what kind of structure is needed for the safety and comfort of the zoo animals.

Investigate: Build the zoo you have planned.

Communicate: Think about and discuss what you might change to make the zoo better.

SORT THE ZOO ANIMALS

Children love animals, but which animals belong in the zoo? This activity will help them to think about where animals belong.

Skills supported:

- Comparing items
- Counting
- Using emergent writing
- Using oral language
- Learning about people and the environment

Materials:

Animal figures or picture cards, including animals that live on the farm and zoo animals

Blocks

Chart paper

Marker

Pencils

Sticky notes

Zoo books (pick one or two):

1, 2, 3 to the Zoo: A Counting Book by Eric Carle

Going to the Zoo by Tom Paxton

Good Night, Gorilla! by Peggy Rathmann

Peek-a-Zoo! by Marie Torres Cimarusti

What to do:

1. Ask children to name some animals that live in the zoo.

2. Show children three or four animal figures or picture cards and ask which ones might be found in the zoo. Hold up each animal and have the class decide if they might find it in a zoo. Sort the animals into two groups: zoo animals and other animals.

3. Read a story about the zoo. Record a list of zoo animals on chart paper. Ask children to help sound out animal names as you transcribe.

4. Tell the children that you will leave the zoo animals chart in the block center. They can sort the animal figures or picture cards and build houses for the animals. Invite them to label the animal buildings with sticky notes.

MOVING AND GROOVING AT THE ZOO

Young children are fascinated with animals. This activity encourages children to use their background knowledge to move like animals.

Skills supported:

- Exploring emergent reading skills
- Developing gross motor skills
- Practicing creative movement
- Singing

Materials:

Animal cards

Zoo animals

Zoo chant written on chart paper

What to do:

1. Ask the children to guess what animal you are pretending to be. Then move like a snake or dog.

2. Tell children that you are going to look at animal cards and see if they can move like each animal. Share several different animal picture cards.

3. Explain that they will learn a chant that they will use as they see different animal cards, such as a kangaroo:

   I'm moving and I'm grooving

   Like an animal in the zoo, oh yeah!

   I'm moving and I'm grooving

   Like the kangaroo in the zoo, oh yeah!

4. Tell children that when you say the animal name and show the animal card, you would like for them to show how the animal moves and sounds. Read the words together, and point to each picture to help children recognize and remember what the animal names are.

5. Ask them to be sure to stay in their own areas when moving.

6. Note that when they are at the block center this week, they can pick a zoo animal and do the chant to show how that animal moves. They can also build houses for the zoo animals.

ZOO ANIMAL VOTE

This activity encourages children to think more about their favorite zoo animals.

Skills supported:

- Comparing items
- Counting
- Using emergent writing
- Collecting and analyzing data

Materials:

Graph with pictures of zoo animals

Sticky notes

Zoo animals chart from Sort the Zoo Animals activity

What to do:

1. Gather children around to talk about zoo animals. Ask them to recall the books you read about zoo animals. Explain that you are going to look at the chart with zoo animals that they previously created. Ask them if they can think of other animals that live in the zoo.

2. Show students the graph with pictures and begin to write zoo animal names next to the images. Say each animal name and give children an animal picture to match with one of the pictures on the graph.

3. Point to the names of the animals on the graph and read them together.

4. Tell children that they will get to vote on their favorite animals, and then you will all look to see which zoo animals are the most popular in your class. Explain that when they visit the block center today, they can each vote for three animals. When voting, each child will put his name on a sticky note and attach it to the graph. Children can look at the graph, locate the animal, and put the sticky note under it.

5. Demonstrate how to vote by placing a sticky note on the graph.

6. Give each child three sticky notes, and tell them they can each vote three times.

7. At the end of the day, invite children to count the sticky notes for each animal. Ask them to identify which animals have the most votes and the least votes.

BLOCKHEAD ANIMALS

Children will have the opportunity to create animals by using different shapes. The book *Color Zoo* by Lois Ehlert will provide models for making animals using shapes.

Skills supported:

- Comparing items
- Demonstrating creative expression
- Developing fine motor skills
- Using geometry
- Listening

Materials:

Blocks

Clipboards

Color Zoo by Lois Ehlert

Crayons, markers, or paint

Drawing paper

Photos of animals shown in *Color Zoo*

Waxed-string sticks

What to do:

1. Gather children around and read *Color Zoo* to them.

2. Share photographs of some animals represented in the book. Ask children to notice what is the same and what is different between an animal in the book and a photograph.

3. Demonstrate how to create an animal picture using different-shaped blocks. Put each block down on the paper and lay a waxed-string stick down around the block to outline the shape. Include faces, ears, bodies, legs, and tails. Ask children to name the animal you are making.

4. Ask children what animals they would like to create. Let them observe animals in the animal books available in the block center. Tell children that they can trace around blocks to create their own animal pictures and use crayons to color the pictures in.

ZOO BLOCKS ROCK!

Children love to see themselves in pictures. For this activity, the whole class will have their individual photographs and names taped to unit blocks. Other blocks will have pictures and names of animals, buildings, and objects at the zoo. They can use the blocks with class and zoo photographs during their block play.

Skills supported:

- Exploring emergent reading skills
- Comparing items
- Displaying self-confidence
- Developing vocabulary

Materials:

An individual photograph of each child

Blocks

Labels for photographs

Photographs of zoo buildings and objects (such as a zoo sign, animals, a butterfly garden, or a monkey house)

Tape

What to do:

1. Ahead of time, take individual pictures of each child. Locate pictures of various zoo animals, buildings, and other zoo objects. Tape them on unit blocks and write the child's name or object name on a label underneath the picture.

2. Gather children around. Ask them to look at the pictures and blocks and tell you what they see.

3. Invite children to raise their hands if they can find their own picture blocks. Ask them what other blocks they recognize. Note that the blocks have a picture of everyone in the class. They also have pictures of other things you might find at the zoo.

4. Ask the children to read the words together. Tell them you will look at the pictures and say each word slowly.

5. Note that when they are building in the center, they can use any of these special blocks with pictures to create a zoo of their own.

USE A BLUEPRINT TO BUILD A ZOO

Blueprints are diagrams that tell architects, engineers, and builders how to construct a building. The children can create their own zoo blueprints to create a classroom zoo!

Skills supported:

- Comparing items
- Constructing
- Developing visual or physical models
- Developing fine motor skills
- Noticing details
- Developing vocabulary

Materials:

Blocks

Blueprints of different zoos (optional)

Dark blue construction paper

Marker

Sticky notes

White crayons

What to do:

1. Ahead of time, build a small structure with blocks on top of a sheet of blue construction paper. Label the structure the Lion House.

2. Gather the children and invite them to talk about zoos. Ask them questions such as, "How does someone build a zoo? How does a builder know what to do? What buildings would we need in a zoo?"

3. Talk with them about how builders and architects use designs called blueprints to show them what to do. If possible, show them a real blueprint. If you do not have a real one, you can find photos of real blueprints on the Internet. Point out that the blueprint shows an outline of the outside of the structure and lines to show the walls, rooms, and doors inside it.

4. Show the children the structure you built earlier. Tell them that you want to make a blueprint of the building design so you can build it again later. Using a white crayon, carefully trace around the outside of the structure. Then, remove a few blocks at a time and fill in the inside of the blueprint with lines to indicate where walls and doors should go.

5. Hold up the blueprint and show the children the parts of the design. Tell the students that you have included materials in the block center for them to use to make their own blueprints. Note that as they make blueprints, you would like for them to think about making buildings and structures for the zoo animals.

6. As the children create blueprints, collect the designs in a class book that they can use again and again.

A ZOO FOR YOU

Children will build understanding of how blueprints are used for design. Children will begin to follow a simple blueprint for a zoo.

Skills supported:

- Comparing items
- Developing fine motor skills
- Noticing details
- Developing vocabulary

Materials:

Animal zoo figures

Blocks and other building materials

Map of proposed zoo with animal houses for most popular animals (one option is the Smithsonian National Zoological Park at https://nationalzoo .si.edu/Visit/zoomap.cfm)

Paper

Pencils and crayons

What to do:

1. Ahead of time, display the proposed zoo map for children to view. Ask children what they think of the zoo. Review the map together, looking at the different types of animals that will live in the zoo.

2. Ask children to use the zoo map as a reference to build a zoo or portions of a zoo using materials in the classroom. They can use blocks, building materials, and zoo animals to re-create part of the zoo shown on the map.

3. Invite children to compare their buildings to the zoo map.

ZOOKEEPER: TAKING CARE OF THE ANIMALS

Children have been learning about the zoo and animals that live in the zoo. This activity helps them consider individual animals and how to take care of them.

Skills supported:

- Using creativity
- Learning about life science
- Using emergent writing
- Learning about people and the environment

Materials:

Art paper

Art supplies

Chart paper

Zoo animal books or videos (try the Zooborns website at http://www .zooborns.com/)

What to do:

1. Gather children around and talk about what things animals need to survive. Note that all animals need food, water, shelter, and space. Explain that when animals live in the zoo, the zookeeper is responsible for them and helps them get their needs met.

STEM PLAY

2. Tell children that today the class will pick a zoo animal to learn about. You can use books and websites to find several zoo animals to choose from. Share pictures, written information, and videos about the selected animal with children.

3. On a piece of chart paper, write *Taking Care of the Animals*, and read the words to the children. Then write the name of the animal and tape a picture of the animal next to it. Point to the animal name as you read it. Ask the children what they know about the animal and how to take care of it. Record children's ideas on the chart paper.

4. Tell the children that the class can learn about other animals on a different day.

ZOO SCENE

Children will love to create a class mural with different animal pictures and buildings.

Skills supported:

- Developing fine motor skills
- Demonstrating creative expression

Materials:

Animal pictures

Butcher paper (long sheet)

Tape

Glue

Magazines

Paintbrushes

Paint and crayons

Child-safe scissors

Marker

What to do:

1. Tape the butcher paper along a wall in the block center so that children can create a mural of zoo animals.

2. When the children are building zoo structures in the block area, talk with them about what they are building. Show them the zoo animals chart from the Sort the Zoo Animals activity, and invite them to create a zoo animal for the mural.

3. Tell the children that they can use pictures from magazines or create their own pictures of zoo animals to go on the mural. Ask them to use the old magazines, child-safe scissors, and art supplies as they each create a zoo animal.

4. Help children attach their animal pictures to the zoo mural. Label their animal or transcribe their words about the zoo.

ZOO TOUR—CULMINATING ACTIVITY

The children will be excited to share what they know about zoos by having a zoo tour! The children will discuss with visitors what they learned about blueprints, animals, zoo design, and other features of a zoo.

Skills supported:

- Playing cooperatively
- Using oral language
- Learning about people and the environment
- Practicing teamwork

Materials:

All of the zoo materials and creations from previous activities

What to do:

1. Gather the children and talk about the zoo that was created in the block center. Talk about what kinds of things they learned about the zoo, zoo structures, and zoo animals.

2. Ask children, "What can you share about the zoo? Will you be a tour guide or a zookeeper who is an expert on animals?"

3. Remind children that they can use the engineering method to solve this problem.

   Problem: Find a way to share your zoo and information.

   Ask: How can you share what a zoo is like?

   Imagine: Think about what we should include in the zoo. What does a tour guide do? What does a zookeeper do?

   Plan: Sketch your plan.

   Investigate: Set up the zoo, and discuss how the tour guides and experts will explain it to visitors.

   Communicate: Do you want to change something, or are you happy with the zoo?

4. Have children organize the zoo center with animals, zoo books, divided zoo areas, and so on.

5. Ask children to practice describing the zoo to classmates.

6. Invite other classes or parents and the community to visit the zoo for a tour.

Dramatic Play Center

The dramatic play center is a favorite area in the preschool classroom. It is a place where children dramatize situations through pretend play, where children gain understandings of how the world works, and learn how to solve problems together. The dramatic center remains an integral part of the learning process by allowing children to develop skills in such areas as literacy, language and communication, math, abstract thinking, and more. The integrated learning approach supports different content and developmental areas to overlap to enhance young children's development.

Dramatic play provides opportunities to connect cognitive skills to real-world experiences. For example, when children are dramatizing and re-creating past experiences, they are learning abstract thinking; and when they are dramatizing experiences, they are constructing their own knowledge through hands-on experiences.

Our approach to integrated learning centers involves designing the proper environment to get the full benefit from dramatic play as it relates to learning. Setting the proper environment requires incorporating a variety of materials from other learning centers into the dramatic play center. Part of the materials list should include items that stimulate literacy activities in reading and writing, such as paper, pencils, wipe-off boards, and newspapers. A cash register can stimulate use of mathematics, and a digital camera can be used to incorporate technology.

Examples of STEM Learning

Science

- Noticing detail—Observing and describing everyday objects to investigate properties of objects using all their senses.

- Comparison—Using certain science tools, such as magnifiers or balance scales.

- Problem solving—Having the teacher pose a problem or set up a challenge so the children can develop a plan to solve the problem.

Technology

- Devices—Providing opportunities to use digital cameras can inspire curiosity and wonder.

Engineering

- Analyzing—Using simple machines, such as ice cream churns and egg timers, to invite hands-on explorations of how machines function.

Math

- Counting—Counting out change in a restaurant.

- Learning one-to-one correspondence—Setting up a table in the housekeeping area with plates, forks, spoons, and so on for each place setting.

- Comparison and sorting—Gathering objects to compare and sort them in the dramatic play area.

Examples in Other Areas

Literacy

- Emergent reading and writing—Letting children work with materials such as magazines, food boxes, cans, paper, and pencils so they can develop literacy skills.

- Oral language—Taking on different dramatic roles, speaking in character, sharing ideas, and interacting with others.

Social Interactions

- Cooperative play—Coming together to play.
- Sharing—Discussing ideas.
- Teamwork—Solving problems together.
- Dramatic play—Assuming and experiencing different roles.

Physical Development

- Fine motor—Using coordination to manipulate items in the area.
- Gross motor—Dressing up with play clothes.

Dramatic Play Center Activities: No Theme

The dramatic play center is a flexible area that can enhance the learning of various content areas. In many classrooms, the dramatic play area is usually set up as a housekeeping area. To prevent boredom and connect the learning goals of your lesson plan to the center, we suggest you change items in this center and stage it during your planning time. For example, if your lesson plan is about the senses, introduce props that will allow you to provide children opportunities to connect to real world experiences. The following ideas can help children extend and expand learning that naturally develops while playing with materials commonly found in the center.

LET'S PRETEND PLAY

This is a great activity to use at the beginning the year when introducing the dramatic learning center. Invite children to share ideas about the roles, activities, and situations they could enact in the center and discuss your expectations for the dramatic play center.

Skills supported:

- Engaging in dramatic play
- Exploring emergent reading skills
- Using emergent writing
- Sharing
- Developing social-emotional skills

Materials:

Chart paper

Marker

What to do:

1. Gather the children and talk about the dramatic center and the materials they will find. Ask them for ideas about what they could do in the center.

2. On a large piece of paper, write "What can I play?" Read the words out loud to the children, and then record their ideas on the chart paper. Some ideas might be retell a story, create a restaurant, and pretend to be a police officer. As you record ideas, ask children to share beginning sounds they might know for the words in their suggestions. Read the ideas on the chart together.

3. Tell children that when they spend time in the dramatic play center, you would like for them to work out ways to share and play with other children. Ask for suggestions about how to play well together. If children do not include ideas related to sharing, roles, and cleanup, then address them with the children.

4. After learning center time, invite children to share what they did when they played.

WHAT WILL I BE TODAY?

Skills supported:

- Communicating
- Using creativity
- Engaging in dramatic play
- Learning about people and the environment
- Developing print awareness

Materials:

Career cards and nametags

Crayons

Glue sticks

Old magazines

Paper

Pencils

Child-safe scissors

What to do:

1. In advance, prepare cards with careers pictured on them. You can cut out pictures or draw your own with a marker. Then write the name of the career under the picture.

2. Remind children that during the Let's Pretend Play activity, you talked about what they might like to play while in the dramatic play center. Show them the chart again. Ask if they thought of any more ideas. Take suggestions from children.

3. Explain that they can look for pictures in the dramatic play area that show people and the jobs they have. Suggest that they might want to act like some of the characters they find. Give the children old magazines and child-safe scissors, and ask them to find and cut out photos that show the careers that they could pretend play in the center. For example, they might pick a doctor, a police officer, or a restaurant server.

4. Tell the children that you will post the career chart in the dramatic play area. Let children glue the pictures they found onto the chart next to the words they represent. If more than one child finds pictures of the career, different pictures can go next to the same career titles.

5. At the end of learning centers, show the chart to the children and read the words while pointing to each picture. To support diversity, explain that people of different backgrounds, genders, and religions could perform the same job.

INTERIOR DESIGNS AND LAYOUTS

Interior designs are diagrams that tell interior decorators, architects, and builders how to decorate a room or a house. Tell the children that they can create their own interior design to help them remember the position of different materials located in the center, to record their ideas about where they could place items, and to remember how to place the materials the next time.

Skills supported:

- Comparing items
- Developing visual or physical models
- Developing fine motor skills
- Using geometry
- Developing gross motor skills

- Noticing details
- Developing vocabulary

Materials:

Blueprint map of the classroom

Geometric shapes

Graph paper

Drawing of classroom centers

Interior design pictures of different rooms (before and after)

Marker

Paper

Pictures of the centers (several copies)

What to do:

1. Before starting the activity, print pictures of rooms that have been enhanced through interior design work along with the original room designs to show before and after photos. Also have a drawing of the classroom layout and icons or pictures to show different centers in the classroom.

2. Explain that an interior designer works to make the inside of a room look nice. The designer might look at the area of a room and decide how to arrange the furniture, predict how people will move in the area, and determine which colors to use for decorating.

3. Tell children that you have pictures of different rooms that show what they looked like before and after an interior designer worked on them. Ask children what they think about the pictures. You might ask, "Why do you think interior designers use the layouts? How do they know what to do?"

4. Explain that interior decorators and architects use designs called interior layouts to show them what to do. Let the children know that you have a blueprint of your classroom, and show it to them. Ask children to find something in the classroom by looking at the blueprint. Call on students to go around the room in small groups to find the different centers.

5. Hold up a picture of a room designed by an interior decorator, and show children some of the different components of the design. Explain that you have included materials in the dramatic area for children to use to create their own interior designs. Tell them they can use paper and shapes to create a design of their own. For example, if they were designing seating in a restaurant, they might want to place plates, spoons, and other utensils on the table.

6. Tell children that once they have created their own interior design, they can put it up in the dramatic play center for others to see.

ALL-STAR DRESS-UP CLOTHES

From jewelry design to paper creations, this activity allows children to integrate the arts into the dramatic play area.

Skills supported:

- Comparing items
- Counting
- Developing fine motor skills
- Noticing details
- Using patterns
- Learning about people and the environment
- Understanding sequence
- Developing vocabulary

Materials:

Card stock or index cards

Construction paper

Child-safe scissors

Pictures or drawings of careers and matching accessories

Glue

Large beads, shells, and other decorative materials

String or ribbon

What to do:

1. Have community helper and career cards prepared ahead of time with matching accessory cards. You can cut out pictures or draw your own with a marker. Then write the name of the career, community helper, or accessory under the picture.

2. Tell children that when they grow up they might be an engineer, a salesperson, a police officer, or even a movie star!

3. Show the children the community helper and career cards, and ask them to find matching accessories or dress-up clothes. For example, a firefighter card matches up with a firefighter outfit and a firefighter helmet.

4. Talk to them about the different kinds of accessories they could create and materials they could use to design the outfits.

5. Tell them they can create career-appropriate accessories, such as hats or necklaces, to keep in the dramatic play center using the assorted materials you have provided.

A STORY TO TELL AND SING

Children love music and stories. This activity encourages the combination of music and stories in the dramatic learning center. Start by reading a book to and playing a song for the children, and encourage children to retell the story song through dramatic interpretation in the learning center.

Skills supported:

- Developing gross motor skills
- Listening to music
- Developing vocabulary
- Developing number sense
- Developing social-emotional skills

Materials:

Ten in the Bed by Penny Dale

Audio recording of "Ten in the Bed" song

Device to play audio recording

Blanket

What to do:

1. Explain that you will read a book that has a song that goes with the words. Tell children that you will read it through once, and then the next time you will sing it together.

2. Tell children that you will make the book and song available in the dramatic play center. Note that the center also will have a big blanket that they can use as a bed.

3. Ask children to suggest ways they can act out the story in the center.

GUESS WHAT I AM?

Skills supported:

- Communicating
- Demonstrating creative expression
- Engaging in dramatic play
- Developing gross motor skills
- Learning about people and the environment
- Using narrative language

Materials:

Career cards

What to do:

1. In advance, prepare cards with careers and jobs pictured on them. You can cut out pictures or draw your own with a marker. Then write the name of the career or job under the picture.

2. Tell children they can play a game called Charades in the dramatic play area this week. Explain that they will pick a card that has a picture of a career on it, and keep it hidden from their classmates in the center. Then they will act out that career for other children in the center to see if they can guess what career it is.

3. Ask for a volunteer, and show them a picture card with a community helper or other career depicted.

4. Encourage the child to pretend to do that job.

5. The other children can guess the career that is being acted out.

6. Tell children that when they are at this center during the week, they might want to play with the Charades cards.

7. Let children know that after they have played Charades, they can pick four cards and create a story about those people.

Dramatic Play Center Activities Using the Restaurant Theme

In this section, you will find various activities that integrate restaurant-related materials in the dramatic play center. Throughout all of the activities related to this theme, children will be working on the overall engineering problem of creating a restaurant.

Problem: Design and create a restaurant.

Ask: What kind of restaurant would you like to create? What kind of food will you serve?

Imagine: Ask children to think about what elements or props they will use to create the restaurant.

Plan: Ask children to draw their ideas on a chart or paper.

Investigate: Allow children to create their restaurant.

Communicate: Let the children discuss their creations and elements of their design. Is there anything they would like to change?

THE TAKE-OUT MENU SELECTION

This activity provides opportunities to introduce the children to different cultures. For example, you could provide materials for the children to stage different kinds of restaurants such as a Chinese restaurant for the Chinese New Year and a Mexican restaurant for Cinco de Mayo. Or the children could prepare a breakfast, dinner, or lunch menu.

Skills supported:

- Exploring emergent reading skills
- Developing fine motor skills
- Learning about people and the environment
- Developing social-emotional skills
- Exploring visual arts
- Developing vocabulary

Materials:

Paper

Markers

Pretend food pieces

Take-out menus from various restaurants

What to do:

1. Gather the children before releasing them to learning centers. Explain that you are going to begin a restaurant theme in the dramatic play center. Ask questions such as, "What kind of restaurants have you been to? What kind of restaurants do you like?"

2. Tell children that you have collected menus from many different restaurants and you would like to look at them together. Read aloud the name of the restaurant from each menu, and invite children to share what food might be offered there.

3. Encourage children to use the menus, aprons, and other items in the dramatic play area to play restaurant together.

MY FAVORITE PLACE TO EAT!

Children will enjoy telling about their favorite restaurants and finding out which one is most popular.

Skills supported:

- Collecting and analyzing data
- Exploring emergent reading skills

- Developing number sense
- Comparing items
- Developing print awareness

Materials:

- Restaurant menus
- Chart paper
- Markers
- Sticky notes

What to do:

1. Draw a column on the chart paper for each restaurant name.
2. Give each child a sticky note and ask them or help them to write their names on the notes.
3. Remind the children that previously they used menus from different restaurants when they were playing in the dramatic play center. Explain that today you will show them the menus again, and they can vote on a favorite restaurant.
4. Show children each menu, and ask them to read the names along with you.
5. Ask children to pick a favorite restaurant and use their sticky notes to place their name under their top choice.
6. Ask children to help you count how many votes each restaurant received. Count together and write the number under each graph column.
7. Have children compare the numbers. Ask them which restaurant got the most votes and which one got the least votes.

MAKE A MENU

After children have begun to play with the restaurant theme, they can now begin to think about their own restaurant!

Skills supported:

- Using emergent writing
- Using technology

Materials:

Construction paper

Digital camera

Glue sticks

Magazines

Paper

Pencils

Child-safe scissors

What to do:

1. Remind the children that they have played restaurant and used menus in the dramatic play center in recent days. Explain that today they will get to start thinking about creating their own restaurant.

2. On a large piece of paper, write "Take-Out Menu," and ask the children to tell you their ideas for a restaurant menu. List suggestions for types of restaurants from children on the paper, and ask for suggestions of what food might be offered at each restaurant. Together, talk about the types of food you would find in the restaurant.

3. Tell the children that they will have the opportunity to create their own take-out menus in the center, choosing which foods to put on their menus.

4. Explain that they can use digital cameras to take photos of the pretend foods or cut out pictures of food from old magazines. They can also draw pictures of food items or cut them out of construction paper.

5. Explain that they can put the pictures or photos on a piece of paper to create their own take-out menus.

6. Encourage children to try to write the names of the foods next to the pictures, if appropriate for their developmental level.

OUR MENU PRICE LIST

This activity provides opportunities to introduce children to math concepts integrating several learning domains. By introducing a price list and play money, you will help children understand the process of paying the bill after receiving a service.

Skills supported:

-   Communicating
-   Counting
-   Using emergent writing

- Measuring
- Developing number sense

Materials:

Paper

Markers

Pretend food

Play money

Toy cash register

Restaurant take-out menus

Child-created take-out menus from previous activity

What to do:

1. Ask children to think about what happens when they go to a restaurant and finish eating. Encourage them to discuss how they have to pay the bill after they finish their meals.

2. Hold up the take-out menus from the learning center, and point out the prices. Ask questions such as, "How much does the food cost? Can you find the prices? Most menus include a cost that is shown with numbers."

3. Work with children to show how much one or two menu items would each cost. Select menu items that will be easy to show with paper money or pennies. Show the dollar sign and explain that it is the money symbol for dollars.

4. Tell children that in the dramatic play center they can add prices to the menus they created. Explain that they can decide how much each item on the menu will cost. Ask them to draw or write numbers with the dollar sign.

5. Suggest that when they play restaurant, they can have one person be the server, one person be the customer ordering food, one person be the cook, and one person be the cashier taking money and putting it into the cash register. Remind the children to take turns in these roles.

RESTAURANT DESIGNS

Every restaurant needs a layout, a visual conceptualization of the different areas. The customer area includes spaces such as the hostess station, the seating room, and the cashier's area. The children can create their own restaurant layout to help them record all their great ideas and remember how to set it up again.

Skills supported:

- Comparing items
- Counting

- Developing fine motor skills
- Using geometry
- Noticing details
- Developing vocabulary

Materials:

Markers

Paper

Table and at least two chairs

Tablecloth

Plates and cups

Silverware

Centerpiece decoration

What to do:

1. Invite children to talk about the restaurant layout and how to set up a table. Ask them how a server knows what to put on a table and where.

2. Talk with children about how servers and architects use designs called *layouts* to show them what to do. If possible, show them a real restaurant layout and pictures of restaurants. Point out that the layouts show how to set up the customer area.

3. Tell children that they will have the opportunity to set up the tables in their restaurant. Ask the children to make the table look appealing to customers. Explain that first they can dress the table with a tablecloth, then they can place the plates, cups, napkins, and silverware in an appealing way.

4. Once the table is set, ask children to draw a place setting on paper so they will have a reference guide to follow next time. Make sure the drawing includes directions for the placement of the plates, cups, silverware, and the centerpiece of the table.

PIGS WILL BE PIGS

The book *Pigs Will Be Pigs* tells the story of a family that is very hungry and finds no food in the house. In this activity, children are encouraged to go out on a money hunt in the dramatic play area, like the pigs in the book do.

Skills supported:

- Listening
- Comparing items
- Counting

- Engaging in dramatic play
- Using narrative language
- Developing vocabulary

Materials:

Pigs Will Be Pigs: Fun with Math and Money by Amy Axelrod

Play money

Restaurant take-out menus from previous activity

What to do:

1. Prior to learning centers time, hide play money in different areas in the dramatic play center.

2. Introduce the book *Pigs Will Be Pigs*, telling children that the pigs in the book are very hungry, but there is no food in the house. Ask for ideas about what the pigs should do.

3. After reading the book, tell children that they can go on a money hunt in the dramatic play center.

4. Ask them how much money they found. Suggest that they can go to a restaurant to spend their money. Ask which restaurants they will choose.

5. Promote turn taking by asking children who have found money to later hide it again for others to find.

WHAT IS A LOGO?

Give children the opportunity to make their pretend restaurants special by using logos. Talk to the children about the definition of a logo. Tell them that logos are special symbols to identify a product or a service. At the end of the activity, children can design their own unique logos for their restaurant.

Skills supported:

- Exploring emergent reading skills
- Demonstrating creative expression
- Developing fine motor skills
- Noticing details
- Exploring visual arts

Materials:

Camera

Printer

Chart paper

Marker

Sticky notes

Magazines

Child-safe scissors

Paint

Brushes

Paper

Glue sticks

What to do:

1. In advance, take a photo of each child. Print these out so each will fit on a sticky note for children to use later for voting. Create a chart with two columns, one for child-created logos and one for votes.

2. Tell children that they are going to explore logos today, and explain that a logo is a symbol or statement that identifies a product or service.

3. Give the children old magazines so they can flip through and find logos. Or you can print out some recognizable logos of companies that the children are familiar with. Discuss the different shapes, colors, and images in the logos you find. Encourage the children to discuss the different elements and characteristics of the logos.

4. Create columns in graph format on the chart paper. Invite children to cut out logos and glue them onto the bottom of the chart paper for later graphing.

5. When children are in small-group time, ask them to brainstorm logo ideas for the restaurant. Ask children to think about the type of restaurant they have created. Encourage them with questions such as, "What colors and shapes do we want to use?" "What is the name of the restaurant?"

6. Ask each child to draw a logo on paper.

7. Encourage children to explain what their logos represent. On the back of the child's paper, write the story word for word as the child explains the concept of the logo.

8. Discuss the different creations with the group, highlighting colors, shapes, and other features.

9. Post the chart in the dramatic center, and ask children to attach their logos in the left-hand column.

10. Invite children to vote for their favorite logo by placing the sticky note with their picture on it in the right-hand column next to the logo they like the most. Discuss the rules for voting, such as placing the sticky note on one logo and taking turns.

RESTAURANT REVIEW

Children will be encouraged to give a review of a restaurant during dramatic play time!

Skills supported:

- Counting
- Exploring emergent reading skills
- Using emergent writing

Materials:

Crayons

Restaurant review forms

Pencils

What to do:

1. In advance, create a restaurant review form with five star outlines at the top and a comments section underneath. Children will be able to color in the stars depending on how many stars they want to give the restaurant they are reviewing. Make copies for all children and bring them to center time.

2. At center time, talk about how people pick their favorite restaurants. Tell children that some restaurants are world-famous for their food, service, and location.

3. Explain that if children use someone's restaurant menu while they are playing in the dramatic play center, they can give the restaurant a review.

4. Introduce the restaurant review form. Note that at the top it has five blank stars. Tell children that if they love the restaurant, they can give it the most stars—five! Count the stars together. Explain that children can color those stars in with a crayon. Tell children, "If you like the restaurant a lot, you might give it four stars. Let's count them together."

5. Further guide the children by telling them that if they are playing restaurant in the dramatic play center, they can order a meal, eat their pretend food, and then review the restaurant by using the form. After they give the restaurant stars, they can write or draw something about their experience in the restaurant. Ask for suggestions about what children might say in their reviews.

MUSICAL FOOD SONG

This activity encourages children to create a musical pattern.

Skills supported:

- Comparing items
- Counting
- Using patterns
- Practicing creative movement

Materials:

Chart paper

Marker

Pretend food

Bag

What to do:

1. Before centers, get a bag and fill it with the pretend food.

2. When you gather the children, explain that you are going to teach them a game that they can play in the dramatic play center.

3. Tell children that they can play the game in the center with one or two other children. Explain that you have a bag with different types of pretend food in it. One person will hold the bag, and another person will pick a food item out of the bag. Once a child has picked a food item, she will get to choose a motion that goes with that food.

4. Demonstrate by picking an item out of the bag and making up a motion

to go with it: "I have picked a potato, and I will pat my hands together three times for *potato*."

5. Pull out a few other food items and ask for ideas: "Who has an idea for an apple?" "Who has an idea for a piece of pizza?"

6. Tell children that when they are playing the game in the center, each person will pick a food item and a motion to go with it. After each person has selected his food item and pattern, the children will set all of the items out in a row and do the motions in the same order.

7. Tell the children that you will try it once now. Use the ideas for motions offered so far, and create a sample pattern by laying the food pieces out on the table in a row.

8. Tell the children that you will write the pattern on the chart paper so that everyone can follow it. Write and draw the following pattern:

   - Potato—Pat hands three times.
   - Apple—Crunch your mouth six times.
   - Pizza—Make an action like throwing pizza dough in the air.

9. Have the children practice making the motions in order several times so that they get the idea.

10. Tell them you will leave the chart in the dramatic play center so they can record their own patterns. Ask them to draw pictures for the food items and their motions along with a number to show how many times they should do the motion.

11. After children have done the activity in the learning center, bring the chart and food items out to the whole group and have them complete some of the patterns together.

OUR LEMONADE STAND

This activity will encourage children to design and build a lemonade stand.

Skills supported:

- Developing visual or physical models
- Problem solving

Materials:

Blocks

Graph paper

Pictures of lemonade stands

Shapes

What to do:

1. Remind the children that they have already been using different menus that restaurants have. Note that they can find different types of food at different restaurants. Tell them that

you know that most children don't have their own restaurant, but they might have a lemonade stand!

2. Ask, "Who knows what a lemonade stand is?"

3. You might tell them a story about making a lemonade stand when you were young and how you sold lemonade right in front of your house. Try to make the story funny and interesting so the children get excited about the idea.

4. Show the children pictures of a lemonade stand. Tell them that they can begin to design their own miniature lemonade stand in the dramatic play center.

5. Remind children of the steps in the engineering method that they can use for this challenge.

> **Problem:** Make your own model of a lemonade stand.
>
> **Ask:** How can you make a lemonade stand?
>
> **Imagine:** Think about what is important for a lemonade stand and what materials you might use to make your model.
>
> **Plan:** Draw your plan.
>
> **Investigate:** Build your lemonade stand.
>
> **Communicate:** Discuss if you want to change your stand in some way or if you like the way it turned out.

6. Show children the graph paper that they can use for drawing their designs.

7. Tell them that after they have created a design, they can build their own tiny version of a lemonade stand.

8. They can review their designs to see if they would like to make any changes to them. Ask them to make sure the model stands up well, and has a place for the lemonade and the money.

9. If possible, leave the lemonade stands set up in a sectioned-off area of the dramatic play center for others to see.

THE BEST LEMONADE MIXTURES!

Children will be given limited materials with measuring items to create and record their own lemonade mixtures. Adult assistance is recommended.

Skills supported:

- Counting
- Measuring
- Using emergent writing

Materials:

Natural lemonade package

Chart paper

Markers

Measuring spoons and cups

Mixing spoons

Paper

Paper towel

Small amount of lemon juice

Small container of water

Sugar packets

What to do:

1. Explain that children can try a special project related to the lemonade stands, but only a few children at a time will be able to work in the dramatic play center. They will get to make real lemonade and taste it! Note that if they don't get to try the project today, they can try it another day during the week.

2. Ask children what they think is needed to make lemonade. List the items that children suggest on the chart paper.

3. Next, show children a container of natural lemonade and read the ingredients.

4. Explain that they can try to make lemonade using water, lemon juice, and sugar with a helper in the dramatic play center. They can use the measuring tools and record what they added. That way, they can create a recipe for other people to try.

5. Let them know that once they are finished making lemonade, they can write and draw about the recipe they figured out.

THE LEMONADE STAND IS OPEN!

Children will enjoy using stuffed animals as the customers for their lemonade stand!

Skills supported:

- Engaging in dramatic play
- Using narrative language
- Using emergent writing

Materials:

Cash register

Lemonade stand

Paper

Pencil

Stuffed animals

What to do:

1. Review the activities related to the lemonade stand. Some children have built a lemonade stand with blocks, and some have experimented with making real lemonade.

2. Explain that you have some stuffed animals that might want to visit the lemonade stand and get lemonade. Tell children that if they play in the dramatic play center, they can visit the lemonade stand.

3. If possible, before center time invite one or two children to tell you a story about visiting the lemonade stand. Record their story on paper and read it back to them for accuracy.

4. After learning centers are finished, invite the children who told the stories to pick people to act out the stories using the block lemonade stand and stuffed animals. The rest of the class can listen and ask questions at the end.

LEMONADE FOR SALE!—CULMINATING ACTIVITY

Children will enjoy having all of their play activities related to restaurants and lemonade stands come together with a lemonade stand in the classroom!

Skills supported:

- Communicating
- Using emergent writing
- Measuring
- Problem solving

Materials:

Lemonade

Chart paper

Magazines

Child-safe scissors

Glue

Paper for invitations

Paper for menu

Trail mix

What to do:

1. The day before this activity, buy or make the lemonade and trail mix. Introduce the activity by saying something like, "I thought we could ask our families to visit our classroom and buy lemonade from us. What do we need to do if we are going to have families visit and buy lemonade from us? What else could we give them?" If children do not suggest trail mix, bring it up yourself.

2. Brainstorm a list of things to do, encouraging children to include the following: make lemonade; make some other treat (trail mix or other); write invitations; gather cups, plates and napkins; and create a menu for the class lemonade stand.

3. Let children work in the center to create the menu. They can find pictures of lemonade and the decided-upon treat in the magazines and cut them out. They can glue the pictures on the chart paper to serve as a menu.

4. Have children do different jobs on the day they will open the lemonade stand, including being chef, greeter, server, and cashier.

Literacy Center

Integration within the literacy center supports the development of a variety of different literacy skills, as books can be a springboard for many STEM ideas. Integrated learning aligns with how children learn naturally; it means their learning overlaps different content and developmental areas. Using open-ended learning centers provides opportunities for children to explore and learn in natural ways! When the literacy center is filled with materials from other content areas, it gives children real reasons and purposes for learning about specific science and mathematics topics. For example, books can provide inspiration for learning in mathematics through hands-on experiences with size and measurement. Science can be integrated as children observe and plant seeds after reading the story "Jack and the Beanstalk." Writing and communication are two important aspects of the literacy center. Providing materials that allow children to express their ideas and learning is central to their early literacy development. Technology is another avenue for promoting literacy, as children's books and related learning materials might be available online or through an interactive application on an iPad or Android tablet.

When considering STEM learning in the literacy area, you can select books that provide inspiration for STEM explorations. It is also important to provide different options for children to express their ideas and learning, such as writing utensils, various types of paper, and digital devices. Technology adds a new dimension as children experiment with recording their ideas through pictures, drawings, and audio and video formats. Also, you can further support STEM inquiry by including related manipulatives in the literacy area.

Examples of STEM Learning

Science

- Science inquiry—Asking questions based on books and investigating.
- Observation—Observing differences.

Technology

- Communicating—Sharing ideas using digital devices.
- Applications—Promoting literacy using books or book-related applications.

Engineering

- Constructing—Creating objects based on engineering principles.
- Building understanding—Learning about engineering from books.

Math

- Measurement—Determining dimensions by integrating stories, materials, and activities.
- Counting—Reading books that provide practice counting objects.

Examples in Other Areas

Literacy

- Emergent reading—Beginning to read books, retell stories, and create new stories.
- Emergent writing—Using invented spelling to label and write.
- Oral language—Asking questions to promote cooperative interactions.

Social Interactions

- Cooperative play—Dramatic play with others.
- Sharing—Reading books and using materials together.

Physical Development

- Fine motor—Using coordination when writing or drawing.
- Gross motor—Moving like characters in books.

Literacy Center Activities: No Theme

The literacy center explores and expands children's inclination to talk and communicate as they learn. Literacy is connected to many different content areas and helps children express their ideas and knowledge. The ideas in this section are integrated but include a literacy focus.

BOOK ART

This is an engaging way to help children notice the illustrations in picture books and integrate art.

Skills supported:

- Communicating
- Developing vocabulary
- Listening
- Developing social-emotional skills
- Exploring visual arts
- Developing fine motor skills

Materials:

Knuffle Bunny by Mo Willems

Not a Box by Antoinette Portis

The Very Hungry Caterpillar by Eric Carle

Markers

Black and white photographs

Child-safe scissors

Glue sticks

Large piece of chart or butcher paper

Old magazines

Paper

Tissue paper

What to do:

1. Tell children that you are going to read some special stories together over the next few days. Explain that while you are reading you would like for them to pay attention to the illustrations (or pictures). Tell them that after story time they can look at the books again in the literacy center.

2. After reading each book, ask the children what they notice about the illustrations or pictures.

3. At the top of the chart paper, write, "What I notice about the illustrations," and read the words to the children. Divide the paper in three sections, and have each book listed in one of the three sections. Ask children to tell you their ideas about the three different illustration formats. For example, they might notice bright colors or black-and-white photos. Record their ideas on the chart.

4. Tell the children that when they are at the literacy center over the next few days, they can choose to make their own versions of the illustrations that they like from one of those books. Before center time, show children the materials they can use for their illustrations. The black-and-white photos, old magazines, and tissue paper are supplied to help the children create illustrations similar to those in the books. However, encourage children to create illustrations in their own ways.

5. After children have explored the different types of illustrations, they can create their own individual pictures.

6. After center time, you can ask children to discuss the ways their illustrations imitate (or copy) those in the books. Encourage them to show which methods they used that are similar to those noted on the chart.

7. If you have space, you can ask the children to attach their pictures to the chart near the book that they used as a model for their illustrations.

IT DOESN'T HAVE TO END THAT WAY

This is a great activity to get children thinking about stories and parts of stories. Children will get a chance to think of a new ending to a familiar story.

Skills supported:

- Using oral language
- Using emergent writing
- Developing fine motor skills
- Developing social-emotional skills
- Developing vocabulary

Materials:

Knuffle Bunny by Mo Willems (book and audio recording)
Device for playing audio recording

Glue sticks

Markers and crayons

Paper

What to do:

1. Gather the children and talk about the book *Knuffle Bunny*. Ask them what they liked about the story.

2. Ask children to think about what happened at the end of the book, when the family went back to look for Trixie's bunny in the laundromat.

3. Explain that if children visit the literacy center, they can listen to a recording and read along with *Knuffle Bunny*. Tell the children that after they listen to the book you would like for them to think about what would happen in the story if they could not find Knuffle Bunny. Ask them to draw and write about what might happen differently in the story.

4. At the end of center time, invite a few children to share what they imagined might have happened differently in the story if Knuffle Bunny were not found.

STORY STONES

For this activity, children will be invited to create story stones that are associated with a familiar tale to support their retelling of the story.

Skills supported:

- Exploring emergent reading skills
- Demonstrating creative expression
- Developing fine motor skills
- Listening
- Using oral language
- Exploring visual arts
- Developing vocabulary

Materials:

A fairy-tale book such as *Goldilocks and the Three Bears* or *The Three Little Pigs*

Markers or paint

Flat, round stones

What to do:

1. Before learning centers, gather children together and read a fairy tale. Ask children to tell about the characters in the book. Explain that the characters are the people or animals involved in the story. Accept answers and point to characters in the book.

2. Tell children that if they visit the literacy center, they can create story stones. A story stone has pictures or paintings of characters from a story. Mention the book you read today, and ask children what characters from the fairy tale they might put on story stones.

3. Explain that children can use their story stones to help them retell the story at another time.

4. Share a retelling of the fairy tale using a story stone to model the practice for children.

5. At the end of centers, invite one or two children to retell their story to the class using story stones.

NOT A BOX

Skills supported:

- Listening
- Demonstrating creative expression
- Developing gross motor skills
- Constructing

Materials:

Not a Box by Antoinette Portis

Boxes

Crayons

Paper

What to do:

1. Read the book *Not a Box* to children. Ask them what they would do with a box.

2. Tell children that in the reading center they can explore different boxes. Let them know that they can sit in a box, stack the boxes, and even imagine that the box is something else.

3. Ask what ideas they have for exploring boxes, and accept their answers.

4. Explain that children can draw pictures of themselves and their boxes. Note that the pictures can be displayed in the literacy center.

MISS MARY MACK PATTERNS

Children love to sing and move when they listen to stories. The story of Miss Mary Mack will help them learn patterns while they sing along with the book.

Skills supported:

- Listening
- Developing gross motor skills

- Listening to music
- Using patterns

Materials:

Miss Mary Mack by Mary Ann Hoberman

Chart with words to the song and the motions

Movement cards

What to do:

1. In advance, purchase or create movement cards. Each card will give the name of a movement and show a picture of a child doing the movement. For instance, jump, touch toes, clap, and stomp.

2. Tell the children that today you will read a fun book called *Miss Mary Mack*. Explain that this story is actually a song, and they can join as you slap your hands on your legs and clap your hands together during the song. Teach children the song.

   Miss Mary Mack, Mack, Mack,

   (slap, slap, slap, clap, clap, clap)

   All dressed in black, black, black,

   (slap, slap, slap, clap, clap, clap)

   With silver buttons, buttons, buttons,

   (slap, slap, slap, clap, clap, clap)

   All down her back, back, back.

   (slap, slap, slap, clap, clap, clap)

3. Read the book with the children, and have everyone do the motions.

4. Tell children that when they visit the literacy center, they can pick two movement cards and do their own movements along with the song "Miss Mary Mack."

MY FAVORITE BOOK

The focus of the activities in this section has been based on several children's books. Children will be able to vote on their personal favorites. The class will then find out which book is a class favorite.

Skills supported:

- Using emergent writing
- Collecting and analyzing data
- Exploring visual arts

Materials:

Knuffle Bunny by Mo Willems

Not a Box by Antoinette Portis

The Very Hungry Caterpillar by Eric Carle

Chart paper to make a graph with the names of the three books

Markers

Large sticky notes

What to do:

1. Before center time, make a graph on chart paper with the names of the three books and space for children to vote with sticky notes above each title.

2. Remind the children that over the past several days you have read *Knuffle Bunny* by Mo Willems, *Not a Box* by Antoinette Portis, and *The Very Hungry Caterpillar* by Eric Carle, and children have been able to reread the books during learning centers.

3. Tell the children that they can vote on a favorite book while playing at the literacy center.

4. Introduce the graph, and explain that you will put it in the literacy center.

5. Tell the children that they can look at the three books again in the center and then vote on a favorite. Explain that each person will take a large sticky note and write his name on it. Then on the sticky note he will draw a picture related to his favorite book. After that, he will place the sticky note on the graph above the favorite book's title.

6. Tell children that after a few days, you will all check the graph to see which book has the most votes!

Literacy Center Activities Using the Theme of Castles, Fairies, and Bears, Oh My!

Integrating the theme of castles, fairies, and bears into the literacy center will allow you to plan activities related to some of the most-loved stories for children. The stories will provide a starting point for children to create their own magical places with their own special characters. Throughout all of the activities related to the castles, fairies, and bears theme, children will be working toward the overall engineering problem of designing and building a magical land.

Problem: Make your own fairy land.

Ask: How can you make a fairy land?

Imagine: Think about the special places in the books we have read.

Plan: Sketch your plan.

Investigate: Build your fairy land

Communicate: Do you want to change your fairy land, or are you happy with it?

WHERE ARE YOUR WILD THINGS?

Children are likely to enjoy thinking about creating new wild things after reading this classic story by Maurice Sendak.

Skills supported:

- Exploring emergent reading skills
- Listening
- Using oral language
- Exploring visual arts
- Constructing

Materials:

Where the Wild Things Are by Maurice Sendak

Chart paper

Crayons

Construction paper

Glue

Recycled materials including paper-towel rolls and paper plates

Tape

What to do:

1. Read the story *Where the Wild Things Are* before going to learning centers.

2. Ask children to recall what happened in the story and what the wild things are like. Record ideas on a chart, and include simple pictures, asking children for assistance identifying beginning letters or sounds.

3. Tell children that when they visit the literacy center in the next few days, they can work on creating new wild things of their own. Show them some of the materials that will be available.

4. Ask children to share ideas for creating wild things. Tell them the materials for making wild things will remain in the literacy center for a few days if anyone wants to make one.

5. After a few days, invite children to share their wild things with the class after learning centers.

WHAT A WILD THING NEEDS

After children have created their wild things, they will compare them to other wild animals and talk about what animals and wild things need to survive.

Skills supported:

- Exploring emergent reading skills
- Learning about life science
- Collecting and analyzing data
- Categorizing
- Using creativity

Materials:

Where the Wild Things Are by Maurice Sendak

Pictures of wild animals

Chart paper

Marker

What to do:

1. Before center time, create a chart with the title "What a Wild Thing Needs," and create columns for herbivores, carnivores, and omnivores.

2. Explain to children that living things need food, water, shelter, and space to survive. Tell them that some animals are considered herbivores because they eat plants, some are considered carnivores because they eat other animals, and some are called omnivores because they eat plants and animals.

3. Introduce the graph about what wild things need to stay alive. Explain that because the wild things are make-believe, we don't know if they are herbivores, carnivores, or omnivores.

4. Show children the cards with pictures of wild animals and the animal names. Tell them that the cards will be in the literacy center this week. Ask the children to look at the animal cards with you and say the names.

5. Note that when children are at the literacy center over the next few days, they can think about the wild things from the book and the wild animals pictured in the cards. They can place one of the wild-animal cards on the graph to show if they think it is a carnivore, an herbivore, or an omnivore. They can also create a picture of a wild thing from the book and write what they think it would eat. They could also think about how it would get food, water, shelter, and space.

WHERE THE WILD THINGS MOVE

In this activity, children will be able to use yoga and movement cards with different poses to retell the story of *Where the Wild Things Are*. They can also create their own stories using the yoga and movement cards.

Skills supported:

- Demonstrating creative expression
- Demonstrating body awareness
- Developing gross motor skills

Materials:

Create your own yoga and movement cards labeled with an element from *Where the Wild Things Are* and a corresponding pose name (see the photos of poses or check out the poses shown on the Kids Yoga Stories website at http://www.kidsyogastories.com/kids-yoga-poses/):

Max—downward dog pose

Wild Thing—downward dog variation

Tree and Forest—tree pose

Boat—boat pose

Dinner—table pose

What to do:

1. Remind the children about reading the book *Where the Wild Things Are*. Explain that you have cards showing yoga poses that can go with the story. Children can use the cards to retell the story by moving and doing yoga.

2. Show students the cards, and demonstrate the poses.

3. Explain that you will tell the story again and hold up yoga cards when that person or thing is mentioned in the story. Ask children to pay attention and be ready when they see a yoga card. Then they can show that part of the story by doing the pose.

4. Tell children that they can act out the story again in the literacy center by looking at the book and the cards, and then doing yoga poses to retell the story.

THE PAPER BAG PRINCESS

The story in the book *The Paper Bag Princess* will encourage children to think about princesses, princes, castles, and dragons.

Skills supported:

- Communicating
- Developing fine motor skills
- Listening
- Observing

Materials:

The Paper Bag Princess by Robert N. Munsch and audio recording

Device for playing audio recording

Paper

Colored pencils or crayons

What to do:

1. Let the children know that today they will hear a story about a prince and princess, but the princess is called a paper bag princess. Ask children for ideas about why she would be called that, and accept their answers.

2. Before reading, tell the children that you will look at the pictures in the story together. Ask children what they see happening in the story, and give them a chance to share their ideas.

3. Read the story to the children.

4. Let the children know that you will leave the book in the literacy center, where they can look at it. They can also listen to an audio recording of the story. Ask them to think about what they might do in the story if they were trying to trick a dragon.

5. Tell the children that after they listen to the story, they can draw their favorite thing from the book.

JACK AND THE BEANSTALK

The book *Jack and the Beanstalk* will be used to encourage children to retell and revisit the story.

Skills supported:

- Exploring emergent reading skills
- Engaging in dramatic play
- Listening
- Using narrative language
- Understanding sequence

Materials:

Jack and the Beanstalk by Carol Ottolenghi

Pretend eggs, colored yellow or gold

Name tags for Jack and the giant

Dried lima beans

What to do:

1. Tell the children that you are going to read the book *Jack and the Beanstalk* today.

2. Ask them who knows what happens in the story.

3. Read the book to the children.

4. Ask children to recall the first thing that happened in the story. Ask prompting questions, such as, "What happened next?" and "What does the giant say when he smells Jack?" Ask the children to say the words with you as you point to them.

   Fee, fi, fo, fum!

   I smell the blood of an Englishman.

   Be he alive or be he dead,

   I'll grind his bones to make my bread!

5. Let the children know that when they go to the literacy center they will find materials that go with the story. Encourage them to act out the story, using the seeds, the golden eggs, and nametags for Jack and the giant.

HOW BIG IS A GIANT?

Children will use inchworms or Unifix cubes to measure a giant.

Skills supported:

- Measuring
- Counting
- Exploring visual arts
- Developing fine motor skills
- Developing number sense

Materials:

Butcher paper

Scissors

Crayons

Unifix cubes or inchworm manipulatives

What to do:

1. In advance, cut the butcher paper into separate shapes to represent the giant's head, body with arms, and legs. Have one set of shapes available at the center each day.
2. Before center time, ask the children, "How big is a giant? Are all giants the same size?"
3. Show children the parts of the giant, and note that you will put them in the literacy center for children to work with.
4. Tell children that they can color the different parts of the giant. Ask what they would need to add on a giant's head (such as hair) and his face (eyes, nose, and so on). Explain that at the literacy center, children can add features to the giant and begin to color him in.
5. Once the giant has been colored, you or the children can connect the parts using tape.
6. Tell children that they can also measure the giant's parts using Unifix cubes or inchworm manipulatives. Demonstrate how to measure a part, and ask the children to count with you.

JACK'S MAGIC BEANS

Skills supported:

- Exploring emergent reading skills
- Observing
- Learning about life science
- Comparing items

Materials:

3 different versions of the Jack and the Beanstalk story, such as *Jack and the Beanstalk* by Matt Faulkner, *Kate and the Beanstalk* by Mary Pope Osborne, and *Trust Me, Jack's Beanstalk Stinks!* by Eric Braun

Crayons

Magnifying lens

Planting supplies: small plastic cups, soil, various seeds in a plastic bag

Index card

Chart paper

Marker

Sticky notes

What to do:

1. In advance, create a card that specifies the steps to plant a seed. Also, create a chart with the title "Should We Plant the Magic Seeds?" Make one column labeled "Plant One" and one labeled "Throw Them Out the Window."

2. Tell the children that when you got to school today, you found a plastic bag with seeds in it. Hold up the bag, and shake it to engage the children. Explain that you found a note on the baggie, and this is what it said: "Magic Beans. Plant me or throw me out the window!" Tell the children that later on they will get to decide.

3. Note that when children are at the literacy center, they can check out the *Jack and the Beanstalk* books and notice differences in the versions of the story.

4. In the center, they can also examine the seeds found in the baggie. Explain that they can use the magnifying lens to look closely at the seeds.

5. Note that after they examine the seeds, you would like for them to record their name on a sticky note, and put it in the column on the chart that tells if they want to throw the seeds out the window or plant one.

6. If a child wants to plant a seed, he can look at the planting card in the center and use the supplies to plant his own seed in a cup.

7. Designate a spot—near a window, if possible—for children to put their planted seeds and observe their growth.

GRAPH OF FAVORITE PLACES

Children will be invited to vote for their favorite places in the books that you read during this theme.

Skills supported:

- Developing number sense
- Collecting and analyzing data
- Counting

Materials:

Where the Wild Things Are by Maurice Sendak

The Paper Bag Princess by Robert N. Munsch

Jack and the Beanstalk by Carol Ottolenghi (or a different version)

Graph with columns for the book titles

Pencils

Sticky notes

What to do:

1. In advance, create a graph on chart paper or use a pocket chart with columns for the three book titles so that children can vote for their favorite place in one of the books.

2. Note that you have been reading books about different places and that some places are magical! Tell the children that in the literacy center they can vote for their favorite magical place.

3. Remind the children about the places they can choose. You read about the land that Max went to where the wild things live. You read about the paper bag princess and how she went after the dragon in his lair. You read about Jack and the beanstalk and the castle that is in the clouds on the top of the beanstalk.

4. Ask the children, "Where would you like to visit? What is your favorite place?"

5. Let them know that in the literacy center they can check out the books that you have all been reading. They can put their name on a sticky note and put it on the graph to vote for the place that is their favorite.

6. After center time, show children the graph and ask them to help count to see which magical place got the most votes.

BUILD A FAIRY LAND—PART 1 OF CULMINATING ACTIVITY

Children will be invited to envision their own magical place and begin to create designs.

Skills supported:

- Creating and designing
- Developing fine motor skills
- Exploring spatial relations
- Using creativity
- Developing visual or physical models

Materials:

Me on the Map by Joan Sweeney

Art supplies

Blueprints or maps

Graph paper

Pencils and other writing utensils

What to do:

1. Introduce the idea that children can begin to think about creating a magical land of their own. It might be like the land of the wild things that Max visited, the castle and woods where Princess Elizabeth lived, the land up in the clouds at the top of the beanstalk, or something totally different that they imagine.

2. Remind children that they can use the engineering method to tackle this challenge. Ask them to think about these steps:

   Problem: Make your own fairy land.

   Ask: How can you make a fairy land?

   Imagine: Think about the special places in the books we have read.

   Plan: Sketch your plan.

   Investigate: Build your fairy land.

   Communicate: Do you want to change your fairy land in some ways or are you happy with it?

3. Read the book *Me on the Map* with the children.

4. Discuss what maps show, and ask children to share some of the features that should be included in maps.

5. Tell the children that in the literacy center they can begin to draw their ideas and create maps for the lands they want to create. Creating a map will help the child outline what

should be included in his magical land. Ask them to think about what they want to include: "Will you have a castle? A forest? A village for people?" Explain that when they create their maps, it helps to think about where everything will go in the magical land. Encourage them to include features such as roads, a stream, or even a beanstalk for traveling—whatever is important to them.

6. At the end of center time, invite children to share their ideas. Encourage a discussion related to creating a magical land.

BUILD A FAIRY LAND—PART 2 OF CULMINATING ACTIVITY

Children will be invited to create a magical place in the literacy center with ideas from the different books and activities.

Skills supported:

-   Communicating
-   Creating and designing
-   Developing visual or physical models
-   Problem solving
-   Using creativity
-   Constructing
-   Developing fine motor skills
-   Using narrative language
-   Practicing creative movement

Materials:

Boxes

Paper

Recycled materials

Tape

Designs and maps from Part I of this activity

Straws and connectors

What to do:

1. Explain that over the next few days children will get to create their own fairy lands, based on their ideas, drawings, and maps created in the first part of this culminating activity. Children can use boxes, paper-towel tubes, and other materials in the literacy center to begin to create their own magical place. Share some of the designs children have already created in the earlier activity.

2. Select a map that was previously designed. Ask the children to look with you and talk about how they could create the land based on the map. Point to different pictures on the map. Ask questions to get them thinking about moving from a map to a model of the land. You might point to a feature and say, "What is this going to be? How can you create it? Where will you put it in your land?" Model this kind of planning with children before they begin working on their own lands.

3. Ask children to share ideas about how they might begin to build a magical land. Here are some questions to think about: Does it have trees? Houses? Castles? What creatures will live there? Allow time for children to create their fairy lands during center time, using recycled materials, tape, straws, and connectors.

4. After center time, invite children who have created a fairy land to tell the class a story, using words and actions, describing what happens in the magical land.

6

Mathematics Center

Children are naturally inquisitive and enjoy learning about the world around them. Math is part of our everyday world, and children regularly use mathematics during their play. When matching up silverware, plates, and cups for each chair at the play kitchen table, for example, they are using one-to-one correspondence. Children develop mathematical knowledge through real-world experiences, such as counting during games and sorting toy animals. The mathematics center provides opportunities for children to manipulate materials to develop foundational ideas in mathematics. Children often use mathematical tools such as measuring in their science activities as well.

Mathematics is integrated into early literacy when children read books, write to explain their ideas, and communicate about math concepts.

Children develop problem solving and communication skills when working in the math center as they build on knowledge and explain their thinking to peers. During

center explorations, they can evaluate the mathematical thinking of others. Provided with relevant materials and challenging activities, children can make connections and apply mathematics to real-life experiences in the math center.

Examples of STEM Learning

Science

- Comparing—Examining the differences between two shapes.
- Experimenting—Investigating what happens when you move a line that is connected to another one.
- Engaging in inquiry—Thinking about how to make two sides equal.

Technology

- Measuring—Using tools to help determine the dimensions of a design or construction.
- Digital recording—Using technology to record data and ideas.

Engineering

- Problem solving—Thinking and experimenting to solve math challenges.
- Building—Using information and data to plan and create.

Math

- Using geometry—Determining how many sides different shapes have.
- Developing number sense—Exploring with objects, such as counting or combining to find the sum.
- Exploring patterns—Using different-colored cubes in repeating order.

Examples in Other Areas

Literacy

- Narrative language—Explaining an answer and defending it.
- Oral language—Talking with other children about their work.
- Written language—Writing the solution.

Social Interactions

- Cooperative play—Counting off for teams.
- Sharing—Taking turns in sequence to use materials.

<u>Physical Development</u>

- Gross motor skills—Moving the body to make a shape.
- Fine motor skills—Using coordination to manipulate materials while measuring.

Mathematic Center Activities: No Theme

The math center focuses on a content area to begin with, but can enhance various other content areas as well. Including books in activities, for example, integrates language arts with math. The following ideas can help children extend and expand learning that naturally develops while playing with materials commonly found in the math center.

DINOSAUR COUNT!

Use ice cube trays or egg cartons to help students develop one-to-one correspondence when counting dinosaur manipulatives.

Skills supported:

- Counting
- Comparing items
- Developing fine motor skills
- Listening
- Developing one-to-one correspondence

Materials:

How Do Dinosaurs Count to Ten? by Jane Yolen

Counting bears, blocks, marbles, and pegs

Dinosaur manipulatives

Ice cube trays or egg cartons

Number cards

What to do:

1. Before children go to learning centers, you can read *How Do Dinosaurs Count to Ten?* by Jane Yolen.

2. Have children practice counting with you. Ask if they can count to ten, then to twenty.

3. Note that the story featured dinosaurs. Suggest that when children go to the math center they can practice counting dinosaurs and other items. Explain that when they count, they will place one item in each section of the tray. They can also pick the number card that matches how many they counted. Demonstrate for children.

WHICH DINOSAURS GO TOGETHER?

This activity will engage children in sorting and comparing dinosaurs and other objects.

Skills supported:

Listening

Comparing items

Sorting

Developing number sense

Noticing details

Constructing explanations

Materials:

If the Dinosaurs Came Back by Bernard Most and audio recording (optional)

Dinosaur counting manipulatives

Small dinosaur toys

Sorting tray or paper plates

What to do:

1. Before center time, read the book *If the Dinosaurs Came Back*, or have the recording available for children to listen to.

2. Tell children that they can look at the book in the math center and compare the different types of dinosaurs to the ones they have in class.

3. After they check out the dinosaurs in the book, they can use the plastic dinosaurs in the center to see which ones go together. Ask children to sort the dinosaurs on the sorting tray or on paper plates. Children may sort them by color, size, and so on.

4. Ask children to tell a classmate why the items in each group go together.

5. Note that they can also look in the math center for other objects and sort them.

BUILDING TOWERS

Children build towers with cubes or blocks to practice counting.

Skills supported:

- Developing fine motor skills
- Developing number sense
- Developing one-to-one correspondence
- Developing social-emotional skills

Materials:

Number cards

Number dice with 0 to 5 written on the sides

Pictures of towers

Snap cubes and blocks

What to do:

1. Tell children they can play a game at the math center. Note that the math materials include a special container that has number dice, snap cubes or blocks, and pictures of towers.

2. To play, a child will roll a die and then pick that number of cubes or blocks.

3. The child will also pick a picture of a tower.

4. The child will put the cubes or blocks together to build a tower resembling the one in the picture.

5. When she is done building, she will find the number card that shows how many cubes or blocks she used.

6. Demonstrate for the children how to play the game.

COPY ME!

Children will create a design using three or four pattern blocks. They will then use words to give instructions on how to duplicate a design.

Skills supported:

- Communicating
- Using geometry
- Exploring spatial relations
- Exploring visual arts
- Developing fine motor skills
- Developing vocabulary

Materials:

Pattern blocks

Pattern-block baggies with the same blocks inside

What to do:

1. Let the children know that they can play a game in the math center today with a classmate.

2. Describe the blocks you are using. For example, "I have four pattern blocks here—a red trapezoid, a blue rhombus, an orange square, and a green triangle. I am going to give each of you a baggy with the same pattern blocks."

3. Tell the children that you will make a design without showing them. Ask them to listen to your directions to see if they can make the same pattern. (Do not show them your design.)

4. Provide directions in this manner: "First, put the red trapezoid in front of you with the short side facing up. Second, lay the orange square above it, with the short side of the trapezoid touching it. Third, put the green triangle above the orange square. Last, take your blue rhombus so that the long side is going up and down and touch the point of the rhombus to the point on top of the triangle." The child will lay out the pattern blocks as you give directions. To help the child finish the pattern, you can give the same directions again.

5. When the child is ready, you can show your design. Ask if the child got the same design as you did.

6. Let the children know that when they are in the math center, they can work with a partner to try to copy one another's patterns. Remind them to use their words to explain their designs.

BUILD A STRUCTURE

Challenge children to build roads and walls with pattern blocks.

Skills supported:

- Constructing
- Creating and designing
- Developing fine motor skills
- Using geometry
- Problem solving

Materials:

Pattern blocks

What to do:

1. Let children know that if they go to the math center, they can try an engineering challenge. They will see pattern blocks that have several shapes. The challenge is to build roads and walls with the blocks.

2. Tell them they could combine the blocks or use just one kind of block. For example, they could use only hexagons for a road. They could use only triangles for a wall. Ask them to experiment with different-shaped blocks to see which one works well for building.

3. Explain that after they build, they can decide if they want to change or adjust their structure to make it work better or stand higher.

Extensions:

- Ask children to make a structure that is ten Unifix cubes high.
- Children can build walls or pyramids and use cubes to measure the structure.

MAKING MATH STORIES

Encourage children to draw a picture or act out a math story.

Skills supported:

- Listening
- Using emergent writing
- Developing number sense
- Problem solving

Materials:

Crayons

Markers

Small books made from construction paper or sheets of paper

What to do:

1. Explain that you are going to tell children a story and that it includes math. Tell them that as they listen to the story, you would like for them to see if they can figure out where there is mathematics.

2. Start the story something like this: "Once upon a time, there was a little girl who had some pets. She had two cats, two dogs, one lizard, and one fish. How many animals did she have?"

3. Ask children to tell you how they can find out how many animals she had.

4. Suggest that some children could act out the animals, or children could use stuffed animals to show each animal and count them. Ask children what they would like to do.

5. Let children know that when they go to the math center, they can create their own picture telling a story with math, and the teacher can help record their voices telling the story that goes with the picture.

6. Explain that you will leave the math pictures in the math center for other children to look at or to read and do the problems.

WHO'S THE TALLEST OF THEM ALL?

As an introduction to measurement, have children organize themselves and stuffed animals by height.

Skills supported:

- Communicating
- Measuring
- Comparing items
- Sorting
- Understanding sequence
- Using emergent writing

Materials:

Crayons

Measuring tape

Ruler

Stuffed animals

Snap cubes

What to do:

1. Ask children questions to get them thinking about size: "Who's the tallest person in our classroom? Who's the smallest person in our classroom? How do you know?"

2. Explain that when you compare the size of something, you are beginning to measure it. Tell children that measuring is when we have a specific number to show the size of something. Let them know that they can measure with different things—with their hands, a crayon, or snap cubes. They can also use a measuring tape or ruler to measure. Demonstrate how to measure with some of the tools.

3. Show the children that you have many different stuffed animal toys in the math center for them to compare, sort, and measure.

4. Tell children that when they are working in the math center, you would like for them to record what they are doing by drawing or writing words.

Mathematics Center Activities Using the Theme of Learning about Myself and My World

This theme can help children use math and other types of skills to think about how they are similar to and different from other people. For example, they can measure their bodies, discuss their interests, and compare themselves to family members.

The activities in this section all support the engineering method challenge of creating a mini-me.

To solve the problem, children will use critical thinking, planning, and inquiry.

Problem: Create a small version of yourself.
Ask: Can you use different materials to make a model of yourself?
Imagine: Begin a list of all possible ideas of creating a small you.
Plan: Decide what materials you might need and what you can do to make a doll like you.
Investigate: Try your ideas.
Communicate: Share what you learned, and decide if you want to change anything or try a new way.

HANDS AND FEET

Use characteristics that children are familiar with to complete this activity.

Skills supported:

- Listening
- Developing number sense
- Counting
- Collecting and analyzing data

Materials:

Ten Little Fingers and Ten Little Toes by Mem Fox

Chart paper

Construction paper

Thick crayons

Child-safe scissors

What to do:

1. Read *Ten Little Fingers and Ten Little Toes* by Mem Fox.
2. Have each child trace one hand on construction paper using a crayon.
3. Children will cut out their paper hands, being sure that each hand shows all five fingers.
4. Discuss how many fingers are on one hand.
5. On large chart paper, draw a line down the middle, and ask children to glue their cutouts in the left column. Write the number five in the right column beside the first hand. Continue writing five each time a child attaches his hand to the chart.
6. Ask the children to count by fives together. Start counting, and point to one hand as you count by fives.
7. Discuss how many fingers each person has on both hands together, and have children count by tens. Start counting, and point to two hands together as you count by tens.

8. Discuss how many eyes each person has. Ask children how you can count all the eyes in your classroom.

9. You might count by twos as you point to each child, or children could use manipulatives or round paper dots to represent eyes.

10. Let children know that when they visit the mathematics center in the next few days, they can use stuffed animals to do some counting. Ask children to think about what they will count on the animals. Let them share their ideas before going to learning centers.

11. Ask if they can count those items by twos, by fives, by tens, or some other number.

MY FEET ARE NEAT!

Children will enjoy reading *The Foot Book* and graphing the type of shoes they are wearing.

Skills supported:

- Listening
- Developing number sense
- Counting
- Collecting and analyzing data
- Comparing items
- Developing fine motor skills

Materials:

The Foot Book by Dr. Seuss

Crayons or markers

Butcher paper

What to do:

1. In advance, use a large sheet of butcher paper to create a floor graph in the math center. Label it "Types of Shoes."

2. Tell children that before centers today you will read a book called *The Foot Book*.

3. Ask children to look around at what kinds of shoes other children are wearing.

4. Show them the floor graph. Based on the discussion about types of shoes children are wearing, add categories to the graph such as sneakers, boots, and dressy shoes.

5. Let them know that when they go to the math center, they can trace their feet and color in what their shoes look like. Each child can put his name beside his shoe picture.

6. At the end of center time, gather children again. Ask them to look at the floor graph. Ask questions such as, "How many sneakers do we have in the class? How many boots?" Ask children to count all the shoes together and make comparisons.

ALL ABOUT ME GLYPHS

Glyphs are graphic ways to organize data; they also allow children to use their creativity and problem solving.

Skills supported:

- Developing fine motor skills
- Developing number sense
- Using geometry
- Problem solving
- Exploring visual arts

Materials:

Sheets of construction paper in purple and red

Precut large shapes—large green and dark-blue rectangles, small yellow and orange squares, and small pink and brown triangles

Assorted colors of paper dots

What to do:

1. In advance, make a glyph that represents aspects of you.

2. Tell children that they will create glyphs to represent interesting things about themselves and how they are the same as and different from others.

3. Show children the glyph that you made about yourself, and explain that a glyph is a way to share information visually. Explain that the legend shares what each shape or color represents. Ask children what they notice about your glyph.

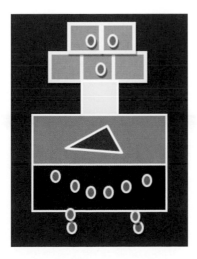

SHAPE CREATURE GLYPH LEGEND
red paper = girl; purple paper = boy
dark-blue rectangle – I like to read
green rectangle = I like to draw
small yellow squares = one per brother; small orange squares = one per sister
brown triangle = I like music
pink triangle = I like sports
colored dots = one for each year of age, select a color you like

Point to all the parts of the glyph and explain what they mean. For example, you might say the following:

I used red paper because I am a girl.

I included a blue rectangle because I like to read, and I added a green rectangle because I like to draw.

I put one yellow square for my one brother, and I used five orange squares because I have five sisters.

Here I have one brown triangle because I like music.

I added thirteen colored dots to show I am thirteen years old. (I am really older.) My dots are purple, which is my favorite color.

4. Ask children to think about how they could use the shapes and colors to make their glyphs and tell all about themselves.

5. Explain that children can use the materials to make glyphs about themselves in the math center over the next few days.

WHAT I LIKE ABOUT ME!

This activity will help children celebrate their differences while they think about numbers that are related to them.

Skills supported:

- Listening
- Communicating
- Counting
- Developing number sense
- Comparing items
- Sorting
- Using emergent writing
- Developing social-emotional skills

Materials:

What I Like about Me! by Allia Zobel Nolan

Mirrors

Chart paper

Marker

Crayons and pencils

What to do:

1. In advance, use chart paper and write the following:

   My smile is _____ cubes.

   My feet are _____cubes.

   My legs are _____cubes.

2. Gather children before center time and ask, "Do you have something special that you like about yourself? Raise your hand if you do." Allow children to share what is special about them.

3. Note that everyone is special and different in your class. Tell children that they can explore how they are special and different by finding their special numbers when they are working in the math center.

4. Ask them to think about these questions: How tall are you? How big is your smile? Do you have big feet?

5. Let children know that they can measure themselves in the math center using cubes and find their special numbers.

6. Show them the sentences about measurement on the chart paper, and tell them you would like for them to measure themselves and record their special numbers.

7. Ask children for ideas about other special features they would like to record using numbers, and offer to write those on the chart paper. Ask children to help you sound out the new words.

8. Children can copy the sentences on paper to fill in the blanks, or you can provide photocopies with the sentences and blanks.

QUESTION OF THE DAY

Children will enjoy answering a question of the day to express their ideas and feelings in class.

Skills supported:

- Developing number sense
- Using emergent writing
- Sorting
- Collecting and analyzing data
- Exploring emergent reading skills

Materials:

Chart paper

Markers

What to do:

1. When the students go to the math center, have a question for them each day that they can answer in graph form. It can be written on chart paper, a chalkboard, or a whiteboard.

2. Introduce the activity by telling children you have added a question of the day in the math center. Tell them that each day they visit the math center they can answer the question by putting their names on the graph.

3. After participating, children can practice counting the answers to see which one has the most responses. Encourage children to look for other names they can also read.

4. Explain by discussing the first question. For example, the question might be: "Do you like ice cream?" The graph would have two columns for the answers: "Yes" or "No." Ask children to be sure to answer when they are at the math center.

5. Sample questions:

   - Which animal do you like better: A cat, dog, or hamster?
   - Do you have any pets? Yes or no.
   - Which ice cream flavor do you like best: vanilla, bubble gum, chocolate chip, or cookie dough?
   - How many brothers do you have? How many sisters?
   - How tall are you?
   - How long is your arm span?

6. Revisit the question of the day after learning centers, if time permits.

AND THE SURVEY SAYS . . .

Surveys are a great way to collect data. Children will love gathering information about their class.

Skills supported:

- Communicating
- Counting
- Collecting and analyzing data
- Developing number sense

Materials:

Clipboards

Crayons

Pencils

Premade and blank surveys

What to do:

1. In advance, create some premade surveys for the children to conduct. For example, "Which movie do you like to watch: *Frozen*, *Aladdin*, or *Tangled*?" and "Did you like the book *Chicka Chicka Boom Boom*? Yes or no." Make copies available in the math center.

2. Remind children that they have been answering the question of the day in the center. Note that it has helped you all gather information about the people in your class. Ask children to tell something they have learned from one of the questions. Accept different answers.

3. Tell the children that today you are adding some special surveys to the math center. Explain that a survey is a smaller graph on paper that they can use to ask other children a question and to collect information from them. Show children one of the premade surveys.

4. Note that when they are working in the math center, they can use one of the surveys already created or make one of their own.

HEAD OF A MAN, MY HEAD

Children will study a painting to find shapes and express ideas.

Skills supported:

- Using creativity
- Observing
- Developing body awareness
- Using geometry
- Developing fine motor skills
- Developing space awareness
- Exploring visual arts

Materials:

Glue

Paper

Pencils

Shapes in different colors and sizes

What to do:

1. Show students the painting called *Head of a Man* by Paul Klee.

2. Ask children what they think of the painting. Ask if they notice different shapes in the picture. Allow children to express their ideas related to the painting.

3. Note that you have put some different-sized shapes in the math center for children to use. Let them know that they can create their own head by using the different shapes.

4. Ask, "Who can help me make a head from the shapes I have here?" Let the children help you create a head together.

5. Ask, "Can anyone change one or more shapes?" Allow children to adjust the head.

6. Tell the children that if they would like, they can use the shapes provided in the math center, arrange them as they would like, and glue them down on paper to make their own head.

MY FAMILY AND ME!

Children will draw a family picture and connect it to math.

Skills supported:

- Counting
- Comparing
- Observing
- Understanding relationships among self, family, and community
- Exploring visual arts

Materials:

Crayons

Family picture

Paper

Pencils

What to do:

1. To introduce the day's activity in the math center, show children a family picture and tell a story related to it, such as: "Here I have a picture of my family. I grew up with five sisters and one brother, along with my mother and father. That means there were nine people in my family! Also, I was the smallest person in my family; everyone else was bigger than me."

2. Tell the children that in the math center they can draw or paint a picture of their family. Note that when they are finished with their pictures, you would like for them to begin to think about the math in their families. They might think about how many adults and how many children there are. They might want to decide if their parents are really big compared to how small they are. Ask for other ideas about things in their families that relate to math.

3. Note that you will come by the math center and check out children's pictures and hear about their families.

THE RHYTHM OF MATH

This activity will invite children to create patterns using different body parts.

Skills supported:

- Observing
- Developing gross motor skills
- Using patterns
- Practicing creative movement
- Problem solving

Materials:

Body-part cards (knees, shoulders, arms, head, and so on)

Unifix cubes

What to do:

1. Show the children how you can make a pattern with Unifix cubes. "I will put down one blue, one white, one blue, one white. Who can tell me what the pattern is? What cube would come next?"

2. Explain that you made an AB pattern.

3. Tell children that they can also make patterns when they move their bodies and make sounds. Show them by stomping your foot and tapping your head, stomping your foot and tapping your head. Encourage the children to try it with you.

4. Ask for one volunteer to think of one other pattern. The class will demonstrate the pattern.

5. Tell the children that when they go to the math center, they can create their own patterns with body-part cards. Ask them to pick two or three cards, create a pattern, and draw what the pattern is.

CREATE A MINI-ME—CULMINATING ACTIVITY

Children will create 3-D models of themselves using arts and crafts materials.

Skills supported:

- Engaging in inquiry
- Creating and designing
- Measuring
- Noticing details
- Constructing explanations
- Developing fine motor skills

Materials:

Chart paper

Marker

Air-dry modeling clay

Glue

Googly eyes

Paint

Ribbon

Scraps of cloth

Paper-towel rolls

Yarn

What to do:

1. Remind children of all the activities they have done related to the theme of learning about themselves and their world. To provide guidance for the challenge of creating a mini-me, explain to children how they can use the steps in the engineering method to plan and create their models of themselves.

   Problem: How can you create a small version of yourself?

   Ask: Can you use different materials to make a model of yourself?

   Imagine: Begin to list all possible ideas for creating a small you.

   Plan: Decide what materials you might need and what you can do to make a doll like you.

   Investigate: Try your ideas, and then decide if you want to try a new way.

   Communicate: Share what you learned.

2. Using chart paper and a marker, encourage children to ask questions related to this challenge.

3. Ask them to think about how they can find answers to their questions.

4. Ask children to imagine how they can each create a mini-me and encourage them to brainstorm.

5. Explain to children that they can plan their creations and then experiment to see how their plans work out.

6. After they have completed their mini-me creations, they can pair up and talk about how they constructed the models.

7. Children can discuss what they think worked and what they might have done differently.

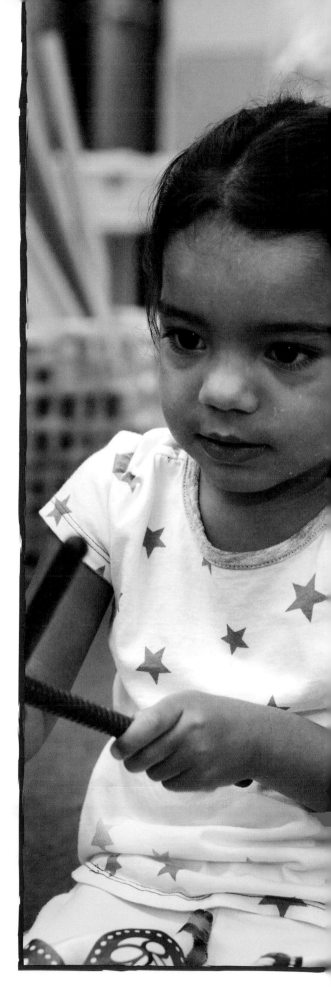

Music and Movement Center

Children love to move, and music can guide them as they move and learn! By integrating music and movement, you can help enhance learning as children use more parts of the brain and develop more neural pathways. The use of music and movement will provide an optimal learning environment to enhance cognitive development. Music and movement can be easily integrated into various learning centers to help children connect with content while being actively engaged.

The music and movement center is a great starting place for integrated learning, because music and movement can relate to many areas of learning and are often a springboard for ideas. Using open-ended learning centers creates ways for children to learn in more natural ways while also increasing focus, attention, and memory. Music and movement naturally include multisensory experiences and can enhance creativity, problem solving, and imagination. The best thing about music is that it supports the development of the whole child and allows children to have fun!

Examples of STEM Learning

Science

- Comparing—Think about what sounds are the same and different.
- Identifying—Determine which sounds are made by animals, occur in the environment, happen indoors, happen outdoors, are made by the body, and are made by instruments.

Technology

- Using devices—Capturing sound recordings.

Engineering

- Constructing—Learning how different instruments are built to make sounds.
- Problem solving—Figuring out how to use tools to make different sounds.

Math

- Counting—Developing the ability to count by singing number songs, rhymes, and chants.
- Patterns—Finding patterns in the beat of music.

Examples in Other Areas

Early Literacy

- Listening—Noticing changes in the tempo or pitch of music.
- Developing vocabulary—Discovering the richness of words used in lyrics to nursery rhymes and songs.
- Emergent writing—Drawing, writing, and cutting out pictures about sounds.

Social Interactions

- Cooperative Play—Playing music and doing movements together.
- Developing cultural appreciation and understanding—Experiencing music from many cultures.
- Exploring emotions—Combining music and movement to express different types of emotions.

Physical Development

- Gross motor skills—Adapting movement according to tempo or pitch.
- Developing body awareness—Singing songs about body parts and different ways to move.

Music and Movement Activities: No Theme

Music and movement centers should have a robust library of music and movement products, including audio and video recordings.

All types of music concepts—such as volume, pitch, timbre, and duration—can be taught. Think about providing products that integrate academics, movement, and music. It is helpful to make small parachutes, bean bags, balls, rhythm sticks, shakers, and all types of instruments easily accessible in the center. To expand the learning into STEM and other areas, children can learn the alphabet, counting, colors, shapes, early math and literacy skills, and so much more. While they move, children are learning the joy of being physically active while developing gross and fine motor skills, balance, and basic fitness.

ECHO GAME—MAKING COMPARISONS

This activity will build on children's interest in games and music while they learn to compare sounds.

Skills supported:

- Analyzing
- Counting
- Comparing items
- Categorizing
- Developing fine motor skills
- Developing gross motor skills
- Identifying
- Practicing creative movement
- Listening to music
- Singing
- Noticing details
- Developing vocabulary

Materials:

Household objects that can make sounds

Rhythm instruments

What to do:

1. Make a sound while performing an action and ask children to echo or repeat the sound and action. For example, hum a long, high sound and reach up high. Ask children to try their best to make a sound as close as possible to the sound you made.

2. Model different types of sounds with actions and have children echo the sound. You can make sounds with the voice, a part of the body, a daily household object, or an instrument.

3. Allow children to be the leader and make a sound with an action.

4. Clap a slow beat (about three to five claps in steady beat). Ask children to clap the same

beat. Try the challenge several different times, using different numbers of claps so children may need to count to repeat. Rhythm sticks, shakers, or other instruments may also be used.

5. Make a sound and ask children if they can do the opposite. For example, make a high-pitched sound so they may make a low sound. Clap a slow beat so they may clap a fast beat.

6. Perform the following comparison song to the tune of "Where Is Thumbkin?"

    Make music softly,

    Make music softly,

    1—2—3,

    1—2—3.

    Play it very loudly,

    Play it very loudly,

    1—2—3,

    1—2—3.

7. Encourage children to continue the song and echo game when they go to the music center.

MUSICAL JARS

In this activity, children will measure colored water to put into identical glass containers. Children will analyze and discuss why glasses with different amounts of water may sound different.

Skills supported:

- Measuring
- Observing
- Comparing items
- Identifying
- Analyzing
- Exploring and experimenting
- Engaging in inquiry
- Noticing details
- Exploring musical sounds

Materials:

Several identical glass containers, each filled with varying amounts of colored water

Measuring cup

Striker (a spoon will work)

Paper

Crayons

What to do:

1. Place the glasses in a row. Fill the first glass container with $\frac{1}{8}$ cup of colored water. Ask children to help you read the measuring cup.

2. Add water to the next glass container with $\frac{1}{4}$ cup of colored water. Strike the two containers and ask children what they hear. Note that you wonder why the sounds seem different. Let children share their ideas.

3. Ask children what they think will happen if you put more water in the next container.

4. Continue to add varying amounts of water. Show how you might make up a song or rhythmic pattern using the different glass containers.

5. Invite children to make up their own patterns with the water containers in the music and movement center. Caution children to leave the containers in place and not to move them from the table.

6. If time permits, allow some children to share their patterns after center time.

KEEP THE BEAT

In this activity children will pat, clap, walk, and perform other movements to the steady beat of a metronome, which may enhance their math, literacy, and speech abilities.

Skills supported:

- Exploring musical sounds
- Comparing items
- Identifying
- Noticing details
- Keeping a steady beat
- Developing gross motor skills
- Moving to a beat

Materials:

Metronome (you can find a simulation on the web or use a program such as Garage Band)

Musical instruments

What to do:

1. Tell the children that you are going to share a special tool with them today. Note that many musicians use a metronome to help them keep the beat when they are playing an instrument.

2. Let them hear the metronome, and ask them to clap to the same beat.

3. Ask children to pat their legs, shoulders, tummy, and so on to the steady beat of the metronome.

4. Ask children to march to the steady beat. See if they can march to the beat while playing an instrument to the beat.

5. Speed up or slow down the metronome, and see if they can keep the beat.

6. Let children know that they can use the metronome when they go to the music and movement center. Note that they can explore other instruments and movements to keep a steady beat while listening to the metronome.

STEADY BEAT—MAKING SHAKERS

In this activity children will make shakers and use those shakers to keep a steady beat to nursery rhymes and music. Using nursery rhymes helps to strengthen beginning reading skill.

Skills supported:

- Comparing items
- Identifying
- Developing fine motor skills
- Developing gross motor skills
- Moving to a beat
- Exploring musical sounds
- Noticing details
- Keeping a steady beat
- Using technology
- Developing vocabulary

Materials:

Audio recordings of nursery rhymes or other familiar songs

Device for playing audio recordings

Empty soda bottles or cans (no sharp edges)

Paper plates

Paper-towel rolls

Pie tins

Plastic cups

Beans

Marbles

Pennies

Rice

Sand

Small jingle bells

What to do:

1. Before center time, play a recording of a nursery rhyme and ask children to join you in patting, clapping, or using a musical instrument to keep a steady beat.

2. Put on a song and create a steady beat with an instrument.

3. Encourage children to tap or keep the steady beat on different parts of the body. For example: Tap head, head, head, head. Tap shoulder, shoulder, shoulder, shoulder. Tap knee, knee, knee, knee. Ask children to share ideas about what body part they could use next.

4. Tell the children that they can make their own shakers at the music and movement center. Ask them to share ideas about how to do that. Let them know that they can say nursery rhymes or play music to keep the steady beat.

MUSIC PRODUCTION

Children will use a software program (for example, Garage Band) to combine instrument sounds using a steady beat. The teacher will demonstrate how to get a steady beat using a drum sound and then will add new instruments. Children can discuss the music, see pictures of the instruments, and move to the beat.

Skills supported:

- Identifying
- Developing gross motor skills
- Listening to music
- Practicing creative movement
- Exploring musical sounds
- Noticing details
- Keeping a steady beat
- Using technology
- Developing vocabulary

Materials:

Garage Band or other software program for music production

Android tablet, iPad, or computer

Drum

Pictures of musical instruments

What to do:

1. Let the children know that they will use a steady beat to make a song. You can start off using a drum or set up a music production application on a computer or digital tablet.

2. Demonstrate how to get a steady beat using an actual drum or the drum sound on a music production app.

3. Explain that you will add instrument sounds one by one to the song. Invite children to play an instrument with you and maintain the steady beat.

4. Tell the children that you will play the song again, and this time you would like for them to add movements and dance to the music.

5. Encourage children to make their own song and music production at the music and movement center. Make the instruments and music production app available at the center.

COUNTING SONGS

Children will use music and movement to help them with counting.

Skills supported:

- Listening to music
- Counting
- Developing number sense
- Noticing details
- Practicing creative movement
- Keeping a steady beat
- Developing vocabulary
- Developing gross motor skills

Materials:

Recording of "Five Cute Roly-Poly Puppies" from Music with Mar. (or a similar recording)

Device for playing audio recordings

Chart

Marker

Other music selections about counting

What to do:

1. In advance, write on the chart paper the lyrics to the song "Five Cute Roly-Poly Puppies" from Music with Mar. (http://musicwithmar.com/) or another number-counting song of your choice.

2. Let the children know that they will get to sing a counting song today. Tell them that they can use movements while they sing the song.

3. Ask the children to hold up five fingers and then pretend to play on the floor like a puppy, along with the words in the song. Next they will hold up four fingers and pretend to play. Continue the song, counting down the numbers.

4. Tell the children that when they are at the music and movement center, they can play the song again and look at the words on the chart:

   "Five Cute Roly-Poly Puppies"

   Five cute, roly-poly puppies were playing on the floor.

   One went outside, and then there were four.

   Four cute, roly-poly puppies were

   Playing puppy games with me;

   One more went outside, and then there were three.

   Three cute, roly-poly puppies were playing with my shoe;

   One went outside, and then there were two.

   Two cute, roly-poly puppies were having puppy fun;

   One more went outside and then there was one.

   One sad, roly-poly puppy was looking for a friend.

   The four came in from outside and

   There were five puppies again!

   ©Music with Mar., Inc., Maryann "Mar." Harman

5. Other song ideas include "One, Two Buckle My Shoe," "Five Little Ducks," "Ten Little Monkeys," "Rocket Ship—Blast Off!"

LEARNING AND FEELING DURATION WHILE COUNTING

This activity provides a fun way for children to develop beginning understandings related to time concepts. They will get practice stomping so that they can understand that stomping eight times takes longer than one time.

Skills supported:

- Counting
- Measuring
- Understanding repetition
- Noticing details
- Developing gross motor skills
- Listening to music
- Keeping a steady beat
- Developing number sense
- Developing vocabulary
- Practicing creative movement
- Using technology

Materials:

Chart paper

Marker

Recording of "Stomp for Each Number" from Music with Mar. (or a similar recording)

Device for playing audio recordings

What to do:

1. In advance, obtain the song "Stomp for Each Number" (http://musicwithmar.com/), or another similar song of your choosing, and write the lyrics on chart paper. You will write the number 1 and then write stomp next to it one time. You will write the number *2*, and then write *stomp* next to it two times, and so on.

2. Introduce the song, telling children that they are going to learn a song and stomp their feet in time with the music. Explain that they will get to move to the song so they can feel and experience *counting* and *duration*. Point to the words on the chart paper as you sing the song.

3. After playing the song through once so that children can stomp along, ask them for ideas about new ways to move instead of stomping. They might suggest clapping, shaking, or moving with an instrument.

4. Tell the children that they can move with "Stomp for Each Number" or another song in the music and movement center. Ask them to make up their own movements, such as stomping, shaking, or hitting their knees, while they play the song. Make the recording available in the center.

5. After center time, allow children to play a game where one person does an activity and the other person has to say the sound and repeat the movement. For example, the leader claps four times. Then the follower says, "Clap four times," and repeats the movements.

"Stomp for Each Number"

Stomp for each number.

Stomp for each number.

Stomp for each number.

One [stomp].

One [stomp], *two* [stomp].

One [stomp], *two* [stomp], *three* [stomp].

One [stomp], *two* [stomp], *three* [stomp], *four* [stomp].

One [stomp], *two* [stomp], *three* [stomp], *four* [stomp], *five* [stomp].

One [stomp], *two* [stomp], *three* [stomp], *four* [stomp], *five* [stomp], *six* [stomp].

One [stomp], *two* [stomp], *three* [stomp], *four* [stomp], *five* [stomp], *six* [stomp], *seven* [stomp].

One [stomp], *two* [stomp], *three* [stomp], *four* [stomp], *five* [stomp], *six* [stomp], *seven* [stomp], *eight* [stomp].

©Music with Mar., Inc., Maryann "Mar." Harman

FINISH THE PATTERN

Feel the steady beat—being able to understand a pattern is a skill needed in science and math.

Skills supported:

- Listening to music
- Using patterns
- Counting
- Developing gross motor skills
- Developing number sense
- Practicing creative movement
- Keeping a steady beat
- Noticing details
- Understanding seriation

Materials:

Chart paper

Marker

Musical instruments

What to do:

1. In advance, write the words to the chant you are using on chart paper to help children follow along.

2. Tell the children that they will get to act out a pattern today. You will say the words and do the motions together two times through. Explain that then you will leave out the last word, and they will shout out the word while performing the movement.

3. Tell the children that you will try it together. Demonstrate by chanting, "one, two, three, four," twice, holding up your fingers to match the number you say. Explain that when you get to four the next time, you will be silent while the children shout "Four!" and hold up four fingers. Ask them to say the words and do the motions with you. If you like, you and the children can practice this sequence a few times before singing the whole song.

4. A song from Maryann Harman has been adapted to create this chant:

   Finish the pattern; patterns repeat.

   It's something we can do that's really neat.

   Move to the pattern; figure it out.

   When we get to the missing word, say it with a shout!

   1, 2, 3, 4 (hold up fingers to match the numbers)

   1, 2, 3, 4 (hold up fingers)

   1, 2, 3, ___ (hold up fingers)

5. Continue the activity with other patterns. The challenge is for children to complete the pattern when the teacher does not say the word. Some examples follow:

   Clap, clap, clap, reach

   Clap, clap, clap, reach

   Clap, clap, clap, _____

   Stomp, clap, stomp, clap

   Stomp, clap, stomp, clap

   Stomp, clap, stomp, _____

   Shake hands in front, back, front, back

   Shake hands in front, back, front, back

   Shake hands in front, back, front, _____

6. Encourage children to play their own pattern games when they go to the movement and music center. Let them know that they can use musical instruments or body sounds to make patterns. For example, a child could shake a maraca twice, and then tap it on his leg (shake, shake, tap).

PLAYING THE KAZOO

The kazoo is a wonderful, easy music tool for young children to try. Playing a kazoo can be instrumental in language development. To play the kazoo, children must push up air from the diaphragm for each sound. This helps to understand syllabication and is great for language development. Playing the kazoo may also get children interested in playing an instrument.

Skills supported:

- Developing fine motor skills
- Developing gross motor skills
- Identifying
- Listening to music
- Keeping a steady beat
- Noticing details
- Developing vocabulary

Materials:

Recordings of "My Kazoo" and "Let's Play the Kazoo" from Music with Mar. (or another kazoo recording)

Device for playing audio recordings

Paper-towel rolls

Wax paper

Rubber bands

What to do:

1. In advance, you can obtain the kazoo songs from Music with Mar. (http://musicwithmar .com/), or you can find other kazoo song recordings online.

2. Introduce the kazoo to the children, noting that it is a special kind of instrument. Tell them that you don't just blow in to it; you hum.

3. Ask children to try making the "do, do, do" sound. Give each child a kazoo and ask him to put the wide part of the instrument in his mouth like a whistle. Ask children to vocalize the sound "do, do, do," making a sound similar to humming.

4. Show children how you might sing or hum a phrase into the kazoo. Ask children to repeat what you did into their own kazoos.

5. Try singing the "My Kazoo" song (or another similar song), asking the children to copy you after you play a melody with the kazoo.

6. Let the children know that they can create their own kazoos when they go to the music and movement center. Note that you have made paper-towel rolls, wax paper, and rubber bands

available for them in the center. Demonstrate how they can put a square of wax paper on one end of the paper-towel roll and seal it by putting a rubber band around the cardboard roll. Show them how they can blow into the other end. Ask children if they think they will be able to make their own music with their kazoos.

> "My Kazoo"
>
> *I like to play my kazoo.*
>
> *And you can play one, too.* (toot, toot, toot)
>
> *I'll play a melody.*
>
> *If you know it, play with me.*
>
> [Teacher plays a melody on the kazoo and children repeat it.]
>
> ©Music with Mar., Inc., Maryann "Mar." Harman

7. Encourage children to play a game in the music and movement center by playing the kazoo along with their favorite song or playing follow the leader with kazoos. Children can also create variations of a kazoo by using different materials.

Music and Movement Center Activities Using the Theme of Sounds All around Us

This theme will encourage children to become more aware of the sounds they hear. During this unit, you will have the opportunity to post a graphic organizer, a K-W-L (stands for know, wants to know, and learned) chart, and children's work, so you can revisit these resources when it is helpful. The activities related to this theme will help children work toward the culminating activity, which is to tell a final story through music and movement. Using the engineering method, children will plan how to incorporate sound, music, and movement to construct a story instead of building a structure.

Problem: Figure out how to tell a story using music, sounds, and movement.
Ask: How can we create a story to tell other people about the sounds around us? What are different sounds we can use to make music, tell a story, and share what we learned?
Imagine: Determine a story you want to tell with sound effects and music.
Plan: Determine what kinds of sounds you will need to complement the music and what kinds of movements you will use to tell the story.
Investigate: Create and practice the production.
Communicate: After practice, discuss the areas to work on to improve the story.

WHERE DO WE HEAR SOUNDS?

Children hear so many sounds every day. Give children the opportunity to think, sort, and classify different sounds by participating in a webbing experience.

Skills supported:

- Listening to music

- Analyzing
- Categorizing
- Classifying
- Exploring physical science
- Exploring emergent reading skills
- Describing and discussing
- Practicing creative movement
- Using patterns
- Understanding sequence
- Sorting
- Exploring visual arts
- Developing vocabulary

Materials:

Chart paper

Markers

Recording of "Sounds All Around" from Music with Mar. (or another similar song)

Device for playing audio recordings

Clipboards

Pencils and crayons

What to do:

1. In advance, obtain the song "Sounds All Around" from Music with Mar. (http://musicwithmar.com) or another similar song.

2. Explain to the children that over the next few days you will ask them to think about the sounds they hear. Tell them that they will get to listen to a song called "Sounds All Around" before center time today. Let them know that when they hear the song, they can join in the words and act out the sounds.

3. Play the song, singing along and doing the motions.

4. Have a discussion with the children about the song and the different sounds used in the lyrics (such as sirens, bells, and a cow's moo).

5. Ask children to think about what other types of sounds they can hear and share them with you. Start a graphic organizer (such as a brainstorming web) about sounds, and fill in children's ideas about different types from the discussion. Some categories for the organizer might be: inside machines or objects, outside machines or objects, musical instruments, sounds made with our bodies, and sounds in nature.

6. As the children provide information, write the words on the graphic organizer where they can see them. They might mention cars, voices, laughter, or dogs. Ask children to give you beginning or ending sounds or letters when listing familiar words.

7. Let children know that they can listen to the "Sounds All Around" (or similar) song in the music and movement center. They can also use clipboards, pencils, and crayons if they want to write and draw other sounds they hear.

"Sounds All Around"

Sounds, sounds, all around (repeating in a round five times)

There are sounds all around and they move right through the air.

Let's listen to some. Tell me what you hear.

Everyday sounds are everywhere. (two times)

This is the sound from a car that says, "Watch out!" (honking sound)

Here's the sound when a fire truck's about. (siren sound)

This sound is made when an airplane goes up high. (zoom sound)

Clocks make this sound as each hour passes by. (tick-tock sound)

There are sounds all around and they move right through the air.

Let's listen to some. Tell me what you hear.

Musical sounds are everywhere. (two times)

Can you name this instrument with strings? (violin sound)

Can you tell me the instrument that rings? (sound of bells)

You bang on this instrument with a stick. (drum sound)

You strum this instrument with a pick. (guitar sound)

There are sounds all around and they move right through the air.

Let's listen to some. Tell me what you hear.

Nature sounds are everywhere. (two times)

Here is the sound of the cow. (moo sound)

Listen to the sound of soft rain now. (drizzle, drizzle sound)

It's soft when walking on leaves on the ground. (crunch sound)

Thunder makes a very loud sound. (clapping sound)

There are sounds all around and they move right through the air.

Let's listen to some. Tell me what you hear.

Voice sounds are everywhere. (two times)

A woman's voice is usually high. (ahhhhhhhhh sound)

A deeper voice belongs to a guy. (boom! boom! boom! sound)

Children's voices sing happily. (ha ha ha sound)

Now use your voice and sing with me. (duh dadda, duh dadda sound)

Sounds, sounds, all around. (repeating in a round five times)

Sounds!

©Music with Mar., Inc., Maryann "Mar." Harman

WHAT WE KNOW ABOUT SOUNDS

Children will share their ideas about what they already know about sounds. You will create a K-W-L chart, using the column headings Know, Want to Know, and Learned. Children will share what they already know, brainstorm what they want to know, and after center time will share what they learned.

Skills supported:

- Analyzing
- Communicating
- Drawing conclusions
- Describing and discussing
- Exploring physical science

Materials:

Chart paper

Markers

What to do:

1. In advance, draw three columns on the chart paper, then label them with the headings Know, Want to Know, and Learned. For the Know column, children will share what they already know about sounds. Then they will brainstorm what they want to know. After working with sounds in the center and during other activities, you can ask children to share what they have learned about sounds and add it to the third column. See the table for an example.

2. Before learning centers, remind the children that on a previous day you started making a list of sounds that they have heard. Let them know that if they think of a new sound, you can add it to the chart.

3. Ask children to share what they know about sound. Take all responses and add them to the Know section of the K-W-L chart. Ask for children to help you with beginning sounds of different words as you write.

4. Ask children what they would like to know about sounds. Place their questions on the Want to Know section of the chart. Ask children to help with beginning sounds and allow them to write on the chart.

5. Note that you will leave this chart in the music and movement center. They can add to it if they think of another question or want to draw something they already know about sound.

6. After center time, you can discuss with children what they have learned about sounds and add those comments to the Learned section of the chart.

What I *Know* about Sounds	What I *Want* to Know about Sounds	What I *Learned* about Sounds
• You hear sounds inside and outside. • You can make sounds with your body. • Animals make sounds. • Voices make sounds. • Musical instruments make sounds and can make beautiful music. • Some sounds are loud and some are soft • Some sounds animals can hear but we can't. • Some sounds hurt my ears. • Some machines and tools make sounds. • Some sounds are high and some are low.	• What makes sounds? • What new sounds can I learn about?	• There are many more sounds than I realized. • Sounds can be used to tell a story. • It is fun to act out sounds. • You can make home-made instruments.

THE SOUND GAME

Children will enjoy playing this game and guessing and describing different sounds!

Skills supported:

- Listening
- Exploring physical science
- Analyzing
- Describing and discussing
- Noticing details
- Drawing conclusions
- Developing vocabulary
- Communicating

Materials:

K-W-L chart from What We Know about Sounds activity

Objects that make distinct sounds, such as a bell, keys, and a musical instrument

Recordings of distinct sounds (optional)

Device for playing audio recordings (optional)

What to do:

1. Before center time, tell children that you are going to play a game. They will close their eyes, and you will make a sound. Ask them to wait until you are done making the sound, then they can open their eyes and guess what made the sound. Repeat the process several times.

2. Examples of sounds you might make are clapping hands, stomping feet, snapping fingers, strumming a guitar, making the sound of a cat, or making the sound of thunder. You can also play recordings of sounds if you like and ask children to guess what they are hearing.

3. Ask children to describe the sounds. This will help them build vocabulary, focus, and notice details.

4. As appropriate, add comments to the K-W-L chart.

5. Tell children that they can play the sound game when they go to the music and movement center.

SORTING SOUNDS

In this movement and music activity, children will identify an object, determine what it does, and imitate or find a way to make the sound of the object. To build vocabulary, children will be asked to use specific words to describe the sound (such as *loud*, *low*, or *shrill*).

Skills supported:

- Listening
- Analyzing
- Identifying
- Sorting
- Categorizing
- Comparing items
- Singing
- Demonstrating creative expression
- Developing fine motor skills
- Developing gross motor skills
- Practicing creative movement
- Developing vocabulary

Materials:

Metal

Musical instruments

Picture cards of other tools

Plastic

Pointer

Song written on chart paper

Wood

What to do:

1. Before center time, have a discussion with children about sorting sounds. Note that sounds can be loud, soft, hard, high, or low. Note that they can find instruments and other materials in the music and movement center. "Plus you can use your own body to make sounds. What are some sounds you can make with your body?" Discuss clapping, stomping, chirping, humming, and so on.

2. Introduce the following song.

   I'm a hammer;

   I'm a hammer.

   Hear me pound;

   Hear me pound.

   Tap, tap, tap, tap,

   Tap, tap, tap, tap.

   Hear me pound;

   Hear me pound.

   Tap, tap, tap, tap,

   Tap, tap, tap, tap.

   Hear me pound;

   Hear me pound.

3. Ask children for suggestions on how to make a hammer sound. You might provide wood, metal, and plastic to experiment. Let children try pounding the materials and discuss how the sounds are different. See which one they think sounds the most like a real hammer.

4. Tell children you will chant the song again together, and they can make the hammer sound when they hear "tap."

5. After chanting the song again, ask children what other objects besides a hammer would make sounds. Allow children to respond. Show picture cards of different sound makers.

6. Let children know that when they are at the music and movement center, they can use the

materials and instruments there or parts of their bodies (such as fingers on the table) to make the sounds to go with the chant. They can use the chant with the hammer sound or pick a new object card and create another sound for the tool.

7. After center time, you can ask children to describe the sounds they made. You can create a chart in advance and record the information they share. An example follows.

Object	What Object Does	Description of Sound
Hammer	Pounds nails	Loud, short sound
Airplane	Transportation—in air	Long, vibrating sound
Whistle	Gets attention	Shrill sound
Cell Phone		
Saw		Grating sound
Siren	Gets traffic to stop	Steady pattern, loud sound

8. You can help build vocabulary by using new words—such as *shrill, nasal, grating, flat, gravelly, gruff, high-pitched, quiet, wheezy, booming,* and *vibrating*—and explaining them.

9. Help children sort them into groups by the sound description. They can use paper and draw graphic organizers such as a tree diagram or wheel and spokes.

EXPERIENCING VIBRATIONS

Children will feel the vibration that produces sound when they put their fingers to their neck while talking and making different sounds. Children will use a recording device to view sound waves and to make predictions.

Skills supported:

- Listening
- Analyzing
- Noticing details
- Engaging in inquiry
- Identifying
- Comparing items
- Categorizing
- Predicting
- Exploring physical science
- Using technology
- Developing vocabulary

Materials:

Recording device, such as an iPad or computer with a microphone

App that shows sound waves on recordings

Drum

What to do:

1. Ask children to share ideas about what they think makes sounds.

2. Ask children to put their fingers on their necks and hum. Ask them to keep their fingers there and say "hello." Discuss what they feel happening under the skin on their necks when they are talking. Accept all answers. Note that what they feel is called a *vibration*. Explain that sound is made by vibrating objects. *Vibrating* means to move quickly back and forth.

3. Ask children to keep their fingers on their necks and say their names. They can feel the vibrations again.

4. Use the digital recording device, and model speaking into it. Show the children how they can speak into the recording device and then see the sound frequencies in waves using the app.

5. Tell the children that they can experiment with making many different types of sounds and recording them in the music and movement center. They can work with another child to speak higher, lower, louder, and softer, and describe if the waves are getting bigger, smaller, closer together, or further apart. They can also experiment with the drum to listen to the sounds it makes.

6. After center time, ask children what they think will happen if you hit the drum hard. Ask what will happen if you tap the drum softly. Accept all answers, and discuss the vibrations that take place. Let them see how the wave lengths change when the drum is loud or soft.

7. After center time, continue to add what the children have learned to the graphic organizer and K-W-L chart.

SEEING SOUND

Children will observe and experience vibrations made using a tuning fork and rubber bands.

Skills supported:

- Listening
- Noticing details
- Analyzing
- Categorizing
- Comparing items
- Identifying
- Engaging in inquiry

- Exploring physical science
- Predicting
- Using technology
- Developing vocabulary

Materials:

Different-sized rubber bands

Plastic container

Shoe box, other assorted boxes

Tuning fork

Water

What to do:

1. Introduce the tuning fork to the children. Ask if they hear any sound from it. Note that it is not moving. Strike the tuning fork so that it is vibrating, and ask children again if they hear a sound. Ask if the tuning fork is moving. Let children describe the sound. Ask why they think it is making a sound.

2. Place a plastic container with about an inch of water in front of the children.

3. Stick the end of the tuning fork in the water and ask children to notice whether the water is moving.

4. Strike the tuning fork on a hard surface so it is vibrating, and stick the end of the fork into the water. Ask the children to notice whether the water is moving.

5. Ask children what they think makes the ripples in the water. Accept their responses, and then explain that what they see is the sound waves or a result of the sound vibrating.

6. When the tuning fork vibrates it makes the air around it vibrate. Any sound is caused by vibration or what we call sound waves.

7. To further demonstrate how vibrations make sound, stretch a sturdy rubber band around a shoebox (without the lid) so that the band has no slack. Pluck the rubber band so that it makes a noise. Ask children to tell you what is making the sound. Accept all answers, and explain that the rubber band moves or vibrates to make the noise.

8. Let the children know that they can use shoeboxes and rubber bands in the music and movement center to make an instrument and look for vibrations.

9. After center time, continue to add to the graphic organizer and K-W-L chart.

WHAT DID MR. BROWN HEAR?

Children will experience rich vocabulary and learn about sounds with the book *Mr. Brown Can Moo! Can You?* Children will also experience sequences and patterns that will enhance math development.

Skills supported:

- Listening
- Analyzing
- Categorizing items
- Drawing conclusions
- Practicing creative movement
- Using patterns
- Exploring physical science
- Understanding sequence
- Developing vocabulary

Materials:

Mr. Brown Can Moo! Can You? by Dr. Seuss

Chart

Marker

What to do:

1. Before center time, read the book *Mr. Brown Can Moo! Can You?* by Dr. Seuss.
2. On the chart paper, draw four columns, and label the headings as in the example that follows.
3. Explain that together you will fill in the chart with the sounds children heard in the book, what type of sound it was, what made the sound, and what movement would go with the sound. Ask children to share a sound they remember from the book.
4. Take children's responses and record them on the chart. See a few examples in the chart that follows.
5. Let the children know that when they are in the music and movement center, they can look at the book *Mr. Brown Can Moo! Can You?* and play a guessing game. One child can make a sound from the book, and another can guess what made the sound.
6. After center time, continue to add to the graphic organizer and K-W-L chart.

What Did He Hear?	What Type of Sound?	What Made the Sound?	Movements and Sounds
Moo, moo	Animal	Cow	Stand like a cow.
Pop, pop, pop	Indoor—bottle opening	Cork on a bottle	Jump up like a cork popping out of a bottle.
Eek, eek	Body Sound	Feet—Squeaky shoe	Walk and make the noise of squeaky shoes.
Cock-a-doodle-doo	Animal	Rooster	Flap your wings and let me hear your rooster.
Dibble, dibble, dibble, dopp, dopp, dopp	Weather	Rain Falling	Show me your rain and let me hear the sound.
Whisper	Body—Sound	Mouth	Let me hear you whisper.
Boom, boom, boom splat, splat, splat	Weather	Thunder	Let me hear your thunder.

LISTENING WALK

Children will listen carefully to the sounds they can hear as they take a walk outside.

Skills supported:

- Listening
- Analyzing
- Categorizing
- Drawing conclusions
- Practicing creative movement
- Developing print awareness
- Exploring physical science
- Using technology
- Exploring visual arts
- Developing vocabulary

Materials:

The Listening Walk by Paul Showers

Paper

Pencils and crayons

Clipboards (one per child)

Recording device

What to do:

1. Tell children that they will take a nature walk and make a list of sounds they notice.

2. Read the book *The Listening Walk*.

3. Encourage children to discuss what sounds were described in the book.

4. Give each child a clipboard, paper, and a pencil or crayon. Explain that you will now go outside and listen for sounds. Ask children to draw pictures or write letters to show what they hear on the walk.

5. Record sounds from the walk so children can listen to the sounds later in the music and movement center.

6. Go inside and discuss the sounds children heard.

7. Tell children that when they go to the music and movement center, they can act out some of the sounds that they heard. They can also listen to the recording to find out if they missed any sounds.

8. After center time, continue to add to the graphic organizer and K-W-L chart.

PERFORMING A MUSIC AND MOVEMENT PRODUCTION—CULMINATING ACTIVITY

For the theme Sounds All Around Us, the culminating activity will be to tell a final story, add movements, and add music and sounds to tell a story. For this activity, children will work on the engineering problem of developing a story with music, sounds, and movement.

Skills supported:

- Engaging in inquiry
- Communicating
- Practicing creative movement
- Engaging in dramatic play
- Problem solving
- Understanding sequence
- Developing vocabulary
- Using patterns
- Exploring physical science

Materials:

Chart paper

Markers

Other materials from previous activities

What to do:

1. Remind children about the steps for solving a problem using the engineering method. Explain how you will use those steps to create a story.

   > **Problem:** Figure out how to tell a story using music, sounds, and movement.

   > **Ask:** How can we create a story to tell other people about the sounds around us? What are different sounds we can use to make music, tell a story, and share what we learned?

   > **Imagine:** Determine a story you want to tell with sound effects and music. The class can write a story with the teacher transcribing it. The teacher can put sentences on each page to create the story. Children will decide what types of sounds they would want in their music story (such as animal, people, homemade-instrument, or environmental sounds).

   > **Plan:** Determine what kinds of sounds will be needed for the completed music, and add movements to tell the story.

   > **Investigate:** Create, practice, and perform the story.

   > **Communicate:** After practice, discuss what you might change about your story if you did it again.

2. If needed, you can provide an example to give children the idea of how to tell a story with sounds, music, and movement. You might ask children to act out the following short story by making the sounds and providing the movements.

   > Our story is titled, "The Day My Neighbor Saved My Kitten!"

   > *One day I was sitting in my room playing my drums.*

   > [Let me hear you play your pretend drums.]

   > [Sing]

   > *This is how I play my drums, play my drums, play my drums.*

   > *This is how I play my drums so early in the morning.*

   > [Play those drums—now stop!]

   > *I suddenly heard my mom yelling, "Oh, no—your kitten got out of the house!"*

   > [Let me hear your mom.]

   > *I could hear my kitten running across the yard.*

   > [Make sounds with your hands showing how your kitten might sound as it runs across the grass.]

   > *I then heard my kitten meowing.*

   > [Let me heard your kitten meow.]

   > *I heard my neighbor open his garage door.*

   > [Show me how your garage door would open, and let me hear the sound of your garage door.]

I heard my neighbor crank up his car.

[Show me how you would sit in your car, and how it would sound as you crank up your car.]

I heard my neighbor blow his horn and put on his brakes.

[Show me how you would put on the brakes, and let me hear your horn.]

Next I heard a knock on the door.

[Knock, knock, knock.]

There was my neighbor holding my kitten. My neighbor saw my kitten in time and was able to stop the car.

As I took the kitten in my arms, my kitten was purring because he was happy and safe.

[Let me hear your kitten purr.]

3. Ask children to think of a story they would like to tell with sounds, music, and movement. Some other examples might be taking a pretend trip to the ocean, watching ants build their homes, touring the zoo, taking a trip to visit grandma, and going for a walk in the park.

4. After children have made up their story songs, let them practice saying the words and doing the movements.

5. Let children put on a live show, or record a show on video for sharing with parents.

Science Center

The science center provides opportunities for children to pursue their own curiosity and interests when they explore natural objects and scientific items. The science center can create a minilaboratory, with many items from nature that allow young children to learn about their world. Science lends itself to integrated learning. Mathematics and science are connected, and children often use mathematical tools in their science activities. Young children also naturally integrate engineering into many aspects of science content and potentially include technology as a way to communicate and record their learning. Children should make connections and apply science learning to real-life experiences when exploring activities within the science center.

Examples of STEM Learning

Science

- Exploring and experimenting—What happens when you mix water and oil?

- Investigation and inquiry—Asking questions and trying to find answers.
- Observation—Looking closely at objects.

Technology

- Recording—Capturing ideas sparked by science activities.

Engineering

- Constructing—Making objects and tools such as a stethoscope.
- Problem solving—Figuring out how to build a structure that satisfies a function.

Math

Sorting—Deciding how objects go together.

Measuring—Figuring out the dimensions of parts of the body.

Comparing—Deciding who is bigger.

Examples in Other Areas

Literacy

- Oral language—Talking with other children about their work.
- Emergent writing—Working to write and draw solutions.

Social Interactions

- Sharing—Working together with materials.
- Playing cooperatively—Acting out scenarios with others.

Physical Development

- Fine motor skills—Tracing objects.
- Eye-hand coordination—Manipulating materials for projects.

Science Center Activities: No Theme

The science center is a wonderful area in the classroom! It encourages children to build on their own curiosity and questions as they learn about their world. The activities in this section will support children as they learn and play in the science area.

I WONDER CHART

Young children have a natural curiosity that can be fostered when we allow them to think of questions, make observations, and decide what questions they are able to answer with regular class materials.

Skills supported:

- Engaging in inquiry
- Using emergent writing
- Noticing details

Materials:

Oh, the Thinks You Can Think by Dr. Seuss

Crayons

Poster board

Marker

Science materials

Sticky notes or paper

What to do:

1. In advance, create a chart using the poster board. Write the words "I Wonder" at the top with a marker.

2. Read the book *Oh, the Thinks You Can Think* with the children.

3. Show children the I Wonder chart, and invite them to share something that they wonder about. As children share their ideas, record them on the chart.

4. Tell the children that when they are working in the science center, they can add a picture or writing to the I Wonder chart to show something they wonder about.

5. Ask if anyone has ideas now. Let children share what they wonder about, and record their answers. If children need help getting started, share some possible ideas: "I wonder why clouds move in the sky." "I wonder why bunnies hop."

A SCIENTIST USES TOOLS

Scientists use tools to learn things and to assist them when they do investigations. Children will explore some tools that a scientist might use.

Skills supported:

- Engaging in inquiry
- Exploring and experimenting
- Measuring
- Using oral language
- Developing vocabulary
- Observing
- Noticing details

Materials:

Children's microscope

Magnifying lens

Measuring tape

Scale

What to do:

1. Introduce children to each of the different science tools. You might say, "Look at what I am holding in my hand. What can I do with this?"

2. Note that these items are all called *tools*. A tool is an instrument that is used to do something specific. Different scientists use different tools, but the tools here can help a scientist find out more information.

3. After children have given different answers, show them each tool, state the tool's name, and explain what a scientist might do with the tool.

4. Tell the children that you have added these tools to the science center. Let them know that when they are in that center, they can explore how to use the tools.

LOOKING CLOSELY

The basis of all scientific work is making observations. Observations are looking very closely to find out more about things.

Skills supported:

- Listening
- Communicating
- Engaging in inquiry
- Observing
- Noticing details
- Developing vocabulary
- Using technology
- Using emergent writing

Materials:

Close, Closer, Closest by Shelley Rotner and Richard Olivo

Children's microscope

Magnifying lenses

What to do:

1. Explain to children that a scientist makes observations. Tell them that an *observation* is when you look very closely at something. Let them know that sometimes scientists use tools to help them look at things up close.

2. Tell children that you are going to read the book *Close, Closer, Closest,* and that each page has pictures of something close. Then the pictures show something closer, and then extremely close using a microscope.

3. After reading, ask children what they noticed in the book. Ask them to tell you which pictures looked different when they were extremely close up.

4. Note that when they are at the science center they can experiment to see what they can find out when they look at something close, closer, and closest. Let them know that you have magnifying lenses and a microscope for them to use. They can also use paper and different pencils and crayons to record what they see when they look close, closer, and closest.

WE GO TOGETHER!

Scientists sort objects to find out what things are similar and go together. Children will enjoy organizing different objects at the science center.

Skills supported:

- Observing
- Noticing details
- Categorizing
- Sorting
- Using emergent writing

Materials:

Leaves

Magnifying lens

Paper plates

Rocks

Seeds

What to do:

1. Explain that sorting science objects is something scientists do. They have to look closely and observe different objects that they find, then they decide how those objects go together. Scientist have created categories for all living things, including animals. They also categorize rocks by how they were formed and what they look like.

2. Explain that when they visit the science center, they will get to be scientists and look at the objects closely so they can decide which ones go together. Tell children that if they want to record how they sort the objects, they can write and draw pictures.

THE PEEKABOO BOX

Children will have the opportunity to use their senses of touch and sight to help them find out what is inside the peekaboo box.

Skills supported:

- Engaging in inquiry
- Learning about life science
- Observing
- Drawing conclusions

Materials:

Seven Blind Mice by Ed Young

Peekaboo box with flap on top, large hole on one end, and small hole on other end

Small items, such as teddy bear counters and small toy dolls

What to do:

1. Explain that you are going to read the story *Seven Blind Mice*.

2. After reading, ask children what each mouse shared about the thing in the book. Also ask if each mouse was correct when sharing an observation.

3. Tell children that they will get to check out something in the peekaboo box in the science center. Explain that they can peek in the smaller hole on the end of the peekaboo box. They can reach in the larger hole and touch what is inside with their hands.

4. One child can put an object in the box, and the other child can try to figure out what is inside the box. Just as the mice in the story had to figure out what the object was, they will figure out what the object in the box is by touching it and by peeking inside.

5. Put an object inside without the children seeing what it is. Demonstrate how to use the peekaboo box.

6. After center time, let the children share the observations they made and how they determined what was in the box.

A TOOL FOR ME AND YOU!

Children will be invited to use the recycled materials in the science center to create their own tool.

Skills supported:

- Observing
- Engaging in inquiry
- Constructing
- Engaging in dramatic play
- Engaging in cooperative play
- Problem solving
- Learning about people and the environment

Materials:

Crayons or markers

Glue

Recycled materials, such as paper, paper-towel rolls, paper plates, old boxes, plastic containers, and milk cartons

Tape

What to do:

1. Tell the children that you want them to think of a problem they have. Ask if anyone is too short to reach the top shelf in the cabinet. Does anyone need help pouring milk in the morning? Are they able to squeeze out toothpaste by themselves?

2. Let children know that tools can help scientists do things. Tell the children that they can invent their own tools that would help them do something. Ask them to think of a problem and then think about what kind of tool would help solve it.

3. Ask for a volunteer to act out a problem. The class will try to guess what the problem is and then give ideas for a tool that would help.

4. Invite one or two children to act out a problem and brainstorm ideas for tools with the class.

5. Let the children know that you have added a box of recycled materials in the science center that they can use to build a new tool.

6. After center time, invite one or two children to share the tools they created and what the tools help them do.

Science Center Activities Using the Theme of All about Me: My Body

Using the theme All about Me: My Body allows children to learn about themselves and the science of their bodies. The theme-related activities will culminate in children completing paper replicas of their bodies showing inside and outside parts.

MY BODY

Children will be excited to learn more about their body and create their own model with the inside and outside parts.

Skills supported:

- Listening
- Communicating
- Observing
- Comparing items
- Developing body awareness
- Practicing teamwork
- Developing fine motor skills
- Developing vocabulary

Materials:

Parts by Tedd Arnold

Large sheets of white or tan butcher paper

Marker and crayons

Mirrors

Scissors

What to do:

1. Let children know that you are going to read a book called *Parts* that discusses the body.

2. After reading the story, ask children what they know about their bodies.

3. Explain that when they are in the science center, they can work together to trace their bodies on large butcher paper. One person will lie down to get traced, and the other will do the tracing. It would be helpful during center time to have an adult available to cut out two body shapes for each child participating.

4. Each child can find another person and compare body shapes. They can make observations about who is taller, has longer arms, or has shorter legs.

5. Children can use crayons and other materials to decorate their cutouts. Let them know that they will get to add parts and decorate their cutouts more completely in the theme's final activity, Putting My Parts Together, Inside and Out.

MY BODY MEASUREMENTS

Children will use standard or nonstandard instruments to measure themselves.

Skills supported:

- Observing
- Developing body awareness
- Measuring
- Counting
- Developing number sense

Materials:

Inchworm manipulatives

Measuring tape

Number chart

Rulers

Scale

Unifix cubes

What to do:

1. Show children that you have a body cutout to share with them. Ask what body parts they can find just by looking at the paper. Note that you can see a head, a neck, two arms, two legs, and the middle part, called the *trunk*.

2. Tell children that they can measure their own body parts in the science center. They can use cubes or a ruler to find out how long their fingers are or how wide their smile is.

3. Let them know that they can write their body measurement on their own body cutouts if they like. You might ask, "What if your hand is 5 cubes long? Where would you write that number?" Tell children that they can use the number chart to help them find a number or they can ask a helper.

4. Let them know that if they are working in the center with someone while measuring, they can compare to see whose hand is longer. They can also weigh themselves using the scale.

THE HEART OF THE MATTER!

The cardiovascular system is central to the body. Children will explore their hearts by listening to them, by doing different activities, and by observing the changes in their heartbeats.

Skills supported:

- Communicating
- Observing
- Counting
- Learning about health and nutrition
- Developing vocabulary
- Learning about life science
- Developing gross motor skills

Materials:

Activity cards

Funnel

Plastic tubing

Stethoscopes

Timer

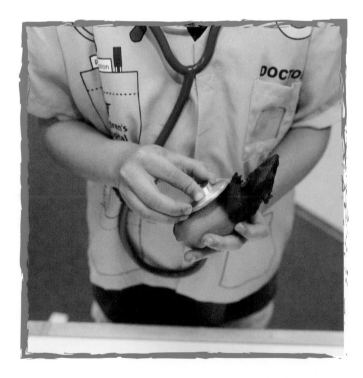

What to do:

1. Tell children that there is something beating inside their bodies that always beats and never stops. Ask for guesses about what it is.

2. Explain that it is the heart, which is a muscular organ located in the chest. Ask children to find the lower center of the rib cage, and then move their hand just a bit to the left to indicate where the heart is.

3. Tell children that the heart is about the size of a fist. Ask them to hold up their fists to provide visual reinforcement.

4. Explain that the heart is an organ that pumps blood all the way through the body to help bring oxygen and nutrients to all the areas.

5. Let them know that they will have the opportunity to try some new equipment at the science center that will help them learn more about the heart. Show them the stethoscope. Explain that when a person goes to the doctor's office, the doctor will use a stethoscope to listen to his heartbeat and lungs. Let the children know that you are putting materials in the science center that they can use to make their own stethoscopes.

6. Tell children that if they find a partner and they are willing, they can listen to each other's hearts with the stethoscopes in the science center.

7. Explain that the process works best if the child acting like the patient sits quietly and then the partner checks her heartbeat. She can then do five jumping jacks and have the partner check her heartbeat again. Then she can do twenty jumping jacks and get her heartbeat checked.

8. After center time, ask children to share what they learned about their hearts.

MY BODY MOVES IN ALL KINDS OF WAYS

Children will have the opportunity to explore how their body moves and connect the movements to different animals.

Skills supported:

- Observing
- Comparing items
- Practicing creative movement
- Developing gross motor skills

Materials:

From Head to Toe by Eric Carle

Chart paper

Marker

What to do:

1. Tell the children that you are going to read a great story, *From Head to Toe*. Let them know that while you read the story, they will have a chance to move their bodies in ways the animals in the book move.

2. Read the story, and then discuss the movements. Ask children to share some other ways they can move their bodies: "Tell me some ways you can move your body."

3. Write on the top of the chart paper, "This is my body, and I can _____ like a _____!" Share your own example, such as, "This is my body, and I can *jump* like a *kangaroo*!" Ask children to share their own examples, and you can record them on the chart. As they share their movement ideas and you record them, ask for sounds and letters they hear to help you spell the words.

4. Ask children why it is good to move their bodies, and acknowledge all answers.

5. Let them know that when they visit the science center, they can check out the book *From Head to Toe*. Explain that they can try to move like the animals in the book, and they can even think of other animals and how they could move like them!

TAKE A DEEP BREATH!

A model lung will help children explore breathing and learn about the respiratory system.

Skills supported:

- Communicating
- Observing
- Learning about life science
- Developing vocabulary

Materials:

2 straws

2 large balloons

Masking or duct tape

Top of a 2-liter drink bottle (cut the bottle in half)

Plastic bag

What to do:

1. In advance, make a model lung. You can find examples online, and one variation is shown on the Nerdy Science blog (http://nerdybaby.blogspot.com/2012/01/model-lungs.html). To make the model lung, put a straw into a large balloon so that it almost touches the bottom. Tape the top of the balloon to the straw so that no air gets in around the edges. Put a second straw into a large balloon and tape it like you did for the first one. Tape the two straws securely together.

2. Place the straws with the balloons hanging down into the top portion of a 2-liter bottle that has been cut in half. Tape around the straws and seal the top of the bottle so that no air can escape.

3. Next, take a piece of plastic from a bag and put it around the open, wide end of the bottle. Use a rubber band to tighten it securely in place and tape if needed.

4. Tape a short string to the bottom of the plastic bag so that it can pull the bag down to simulate breath coming into the respiratory system.

5. Try it out before showing it to the children. If the model does not work at first, try taping it up further to make sure it is airtight.

6. When you introduce the model lungs, explain to the children that the plastic bottle represents the rib cage, the balloons represent the lungs, the straws represent the trachea, and the plastic bag represents the diaphragm.

7. Tell children that their respiratory system has different parts, but the main part is the lungs. Ask everyone to take a deep breath. Ask what they notice.

8. When you take a deep breath, your lungs expand as they take in air. As you exhale, you release the air out again and start over.

9. Demonstrate simulated breathing with the model lung, so the children can watch the lungs expand.

10. Tell the children that when they visit the science center they can check out the model lung and explore how the respiratory system or breathing system works.

11. Let children know that when they are using the respiratory system, they can make observations about what happens in the model.

12. In the science center, children can also create a pair of lungs to put on their body cutouts. They can tell another child about how the respiratory system works.

BONES, BONES, BONES ENGINEERING CHALLENGE

Children will get to explore X-rays to help them learn about bones. They will also be invited to complete an engineering challenge to help a floppy doll stand up.

Skills supported:

- Listening
- Observing
- Counting
- Comparing items
- Engaging in inquiry
- Learning about life science

Materials:

Bones: Skeletons and How They Work by Steve Jenkins

Masking tape

Paper-towel rolls

Popsicle sticks

Cotton swabs

X-rays

Cloth dolls

What to do:

1. Read the story *Bones: Skeletons and How They Work*.

2. Ask children if they can tell you why humans and animals have bones.

3. Show the children an X-ray, and let them know that they can check out X-rays in the science center. Ask them to make careful observations and count how many bones they see.

4. Let them know that you have also put some cloth dolls in the science center. If children would like a challenge, they can use different materials to help the dolls stand up. Explain that children need bones to stand up. Note that the dolls will be floppy unless children give them some kind of support.

5. Ask children to share ideas about what they could use to help the dolls stand tall.

6. Remind children that they can use the engineering method to solve this problem.

   Problem: Find a way to make a cloth doll stand up.

   Ask: How can you help the doll stand up?

   Imagine: Think about what the doll needs to be able to stand. How can you create a skeletal system for a doll? Think of possible ways.

   Plan: Sketch your plan.

   Investigate: Build your skeleton for the doll. See how it works.

   Communicate: Share what you have learned. Decide if you want to change something or if you are happy with the way your doll stands.

PUTTING MY PARTS TOGETHER: INSIDE AND OUT—CULMINATING ACTIVITY

Children will revisit their body cutouts and add features. They can add different parts they have learned about to the inside of the cutouts. They can also add hair and clothes, and decorate their bodies on the outside.

Skills supported:

- Observing
- Engaging in inquiry
- Constructing explanations
- Learning about health and nutrition
- Developing body awareness

Materials:

Cutouts of body parts explored in previous activities (such as teeth and lungs)

Cloth scraps

Construction paper

Crayons

Glue

Yarn

Visual of body with internal parts showing

What to do:

1. Discuss with children what they have been learning about their bodies, how they move, and the different parts of their bodies or systems that help them be healthy.

2. Let children know that they can work on their body cutouts when they visit the science center. They will be able to do two things to decorate their body cutouts.

3. They can think about what is inside their bodies and add some of those parts. Ask children to share what they learned about that is inside the body. Point to the visual showing internal parts to help children remember.

4. They can also think about what is on the outside of the body. Ask children to name some of the features they see on the outside of their bodies. Let them know that they can begin to add hair, eyes, clothes, and draw in other parts of the body. Tell children that they may find that they need more than one day to decorate their bodies.

5. Let the children know that in the coming week, they will invite their families into the classroom so children can share what they know and have learned about their bodies!

Assessing and Enhancing Children's Thinking and Understanding in Learning Centers

Play during learning centers provides a natural and motivating activity for young children in the classroom. Although play is a time of learning, it also provides a window into children's developmental levels. Children's play provides opportunities for valuable teaching and learning, and for assessment of children's learning and development. By observing children's play in learning centers, you can conduct formative assessments to identify children's strengths and weaknesses and to help you plan activities that can enhance their skills as needed.

Assessing Developmental and Content Areas

You may have general goals for children involved in play associated with their social interactions and development. Look for specific developmental domains to assess. Consider the children's engagement with materials in purposeful activities during play. For starters, you might look for the following behaviors as you assess children's play:

- Engages in play.
- Shows initiative and curiosity during play.
- Maintains a play theme.
- Will play for ten or more minutes on one topic.
- Interacts with one or more children during a play theme.
- Negotiates play themes with one or more children.

Additionally, children's social interactions during play provide insights into their ability to initiate and extend social play. Are children able to enter into a group playing in the classroom? Can children express their ideas for activities with others and negotiate roles during play? Are children able to negotiate story lines with others? What type of language does the child use during play? Language is central for children as they communicate and interact with others during play. Children commonly use language to share their ideas related to play themes, to initiate play, and to negotiate roles during play. Narrative language is used as children tell stories associated with their play. When assessing children's language and literacy skills during play, you might look for the following behaviors:

- Uses imaginary objects during play.
- Uses words to create a play scene.
- Uses language to communicate needs.
- Uses language to encourage others during play.

Play includes benefits related to social interactions with children. It also supports children's persistence and engagement in play. Play supports children's use of language. Beyond these areas, play in learning centers can provide a platform for children to learn different content including science, technology, engineering, and mathematics.

Using Portfolios

One significant way to track children's progress and development during learning centers is through the use of portfolios. You and the child should create this record, which is a collection of various artifacts representing the child's educational experience over time to show progress. Portfolios can include pictures of the children engaged in activities, transcriptions of the children's words to explain what they are doing or their learning on a certain topic, running records, anecdotal records, video and audio recordings, student writing or pictures, work samples, and other materials.

As you observe children's play in learning centers, you may want to look for certain behaviors and associated learning. The chart on page 164 provides a list of developmental and content areas that can serve as a reference and guide while assessing play in centers. You may wish to use it to create a record of observations that you can include in children's portfolios and use for formative assessment. The chart can serve as a checklist to review specific learning items children have mastered. Include the date a child has demonstrated or mastered learning on the side of the chart to track student progress. Additional comments could be added to note interesting or unique observations.

The observation form on page 165 can also be printed and available during play time as a recording device and can be added to the portfolio with other evidence and documentation.

The Teacher's Role in Play During Learning Centers

The teacher's role during play can enhance children's learning and interactions with materials and ideas. The teacher is a major factor in learning centers. The teacher can be involved at various levels depending on the needs of the students.

- Assist with problem solving
- Redirect children
- Ask questions
- Initiate feedback loops
- Provide information
- Entice play themes

Teachers are a crucial element in children's learning. Teachers initially observe and assess through observations, but teachers' interactions can support, enhance, and scaffold learning during play.

Next Steps: How to Integrate Additional Topics

Where do you go from here? If you are interested in creating more theme activities and lessons to enhance your learning centers, think about some of the specific themes you have used in your classroom. Creating themes that add materials and activities for your existing centers can bring new excitement and energy to the classroom.

Identify a Theme

To get started, identify a theme that you would like to include in a specific center. Many themes can be accomplished in different learning centers, although some themes seem to create a stronger match with specific learning centers. The block center is a great match for many building themes such as bridges, houses, and cities. The mathematics center lends itself to different themes that would include measurement and counting, such as an animal theme.

Content or Developmental Area	Behavior	Demonstrated Learning
Science	• Asks questions and makes predictions • Observes and experiments • Evaluates and communicates results	• Demonstrates the use of simple tools and equipment for observing and investigating • Examines objects and makes comparisons • Identifies the characteristics of living things • Identifies the five senses and explores functions of each
Technology	• Explores technology • Uses technology to enhance learning	• Explores interactive technology • Uses touch screens • Begins to use applications to record ideas through pictures, drawings, and talking
Engineering	• Identifies problems • Brainstorms solutions • Initiates a plan • Revisits the problem	• Asks questions, identifies problems • Can consider several solutions • Initiates a plan to solve a problem • Reflects on plan to see if it met the goals and/or solved the problem • Revises and redesigns
Mathematics	• Explores number concepts • Uses geometry • Explores spatial awareness • Sorts and compares	• Uses number sense during play, including counting objects and items • Identifies shapes when using blocks or other materials • Demonstrates understanding of spatial awareness concepts such as over, under, between, and beside
Language and Literacy	• Develops communication skills • Develops emergent literacy skills	• Uses language to communicate ideas
Social-Emotional	• Has appropriate interactions with others • Shows self-regulation	• Interacts with peers appropriately • Interacts with adults appropriately • Can recover from anger and be cooperative • Verbalizes emotions • Maintains a stable temperament • Differentiates between fact and fantasy
Art, Music, and Creativity	• Uses elements of arts, music, and creativity	• Shows understanding of beginning ideas related to the elements of art: color, value, line, shape, form, texture, and space • Shows understanding of beginning ideas related to music, including loud, soft, slow, fast, and patterns • Can respond to music by talking and drawing • Uses art supplies to create lines and shapes • Can draw a person as a sun face with arms and legs • Can draw animals, trees, and flowers • Draws multiple objects together in a picture
Fine Motor Skills	• Engages in movements and actions with hands	• Cuts paper • Draws a circle • Builds with blocks and other building toys • Strings beads
Gross Motor Skills	• Engages in movements involving the larger, stronger muscle groups	• Balances on one foot; runs around obstacles • Skips • Walks up and down stairs, alternating feet • Throws ball

Student Name: _____

Date: _____

Focus of Observation: _____

Learning Center Observed: _____

Science Observations

_____ Demonstrates the use of simple tools and equipment for observing and investigating

_____ Examines objects and makes comparisons

_____ Identifies the characteristics of living things

_____ Identifies the five senses and explores functions of each

Technology Observations

_____ Explores interactive technology

_____ Uses touch screens

_____ Begins to use applications to record ideas through pictures, drawings, talking

Engineering Observations

_____ Asks questions, identifies problems

_____ Can consider several solutions

_____ Initiates a plan to solve a problem

_____ Reflects on plan to see if it met the goals and/or solved the problem

_____ Revises and redesigns

Mathematics Observations

_____ Uses number sense during play, including counting objects and items

_____ Identifies shapes when using blocks or other materials

_____ Can understand spatial awareness concepts, such as over, under, between, beside, etc.

Language and Literacy Observations

_____ Uses language to communicate ideas

_____ Communicates wants and needs to others

_____ Models reading a book

_____ Uses narrative language to tell stories such as once upon a time, and then, the end

_____ Makes up or retells a story

_____ Prints own name

_____ Scribbles and letters to represent words

Social-Emotional Observations

_____ Interacts with peers appropriately

_____ Interacts with adults appropriately

_____ Is able to recover from anger and be cooperative

_____ Verbalizes emotions

_____ Maintains a stable temperament

_____ Differentiates between fact and fantasy

Art, Music, and Creativity Observations

_____ Shows understanding of beginning ideas related to the elements of art: color, value, line, shape, form, texture, and space

_____ Shows understanding of beginning ideas related to music, including loud and soft, slow and fast, patterns

_____ Can respond to music by talking and drawing

_____ Uses art supplies to create lines and shapes

_____ Can draw a person as sun face with arms and legs

_____ Can draw animals, trees, flowers

_____ Draws multiple objects together in a picture

Fine Motor Skills Observations

_____ Cuts paper

_____ Draws a circle

_____ Builds with blocks and other building toys

_____ Strings beads

Gross Motor Skills Observations

_____ Balances on one foot, run around obstacles

_____ Skips

_____ Walks up and down stairs alternating feet

_____ Throws ball

Other Areas Observations: _____

Comments and Summary: _____

Strengths and Weaknesses: _____

Recommendations: _____

Teacher/Class: _____

Common themes in preschool learning:

- Back to school
- Beach
- Circus
- Community helpers
- Dinosaurs
- Family
- Farm
- Five senses
- Friendship
- Gardening
- Insects
- Jungle
- Nursery rhymes
- Ocean
- Pets
- Plants
- Seasons
- Teddy bears
- Transportation
- Weather

Planning to Integrate the Theme

When brainstorming a certain topic, begin to think about the natural integration that can occur within the following areas:

- Science
- Technology
- Engineering
- Mathematics
- Literacy
- Music and movement
- Dramatic play
- Social and emotional development

Brainstorm specific activities that could be accomplished in a learning center and could have the potential for integration. Using a graphic organizer, such as the one that follows, is a helpful way to consider various content areas.

Graphic Organizer for Brainstorming

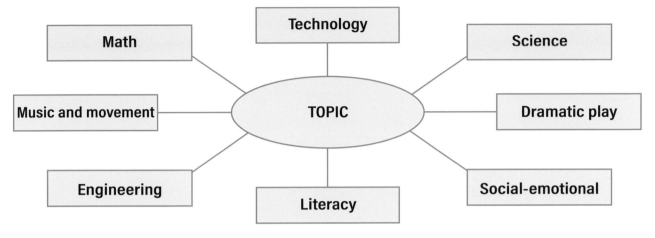

Consider the following skills that may be accomplished through various activities and learning centers. Check off skills and content areas that apply to individual lessons.

Science, Technology, Engineering, and Math

Science
_____ Learning about earth and space
_____ Learning about people and the environment
_____ Learning about health and nutrition
_____ Engaging in inquiry and investigation
_____ Learning about life science
_____ Exploring physical science
_____ Properties of matter
_____ Sound

Technology
_____ Exploring the functions of technology tools
_____ Using technology tools to communicate

Engineering
_____ Constructing
_____ Developing visual or physical models

Math
_____ Counting
_____ Using geometry (shapes)
_____ Measuring

_____ Developing number sense
_____ Developing one-to-one correspondence
_____ Using patterns
_____ Understanding sequence
_____ Sorting
_____ Exploring spatial relations

STEM Thinking

_____ Analyzing
_____ Categorizing
_____ Classifying
_____ Comparing
_____ Drawing conclusions
_____ Constructing explanations
_____ Creating and designing
_____ Collecting and analyzing data
_____ Exploring and experimenting
_____ Identifying
_____ Engaging in inquiry
_____ Noticing details
_____ Observing
_____ Making predictions
_____ Solving problems

Early Literacy

_____ Communicating
_____ Demonstrating creative expression
_____ Exploring emergent reading skills
_____ Using emergent writing
_____ Listening
_____ Using narrative language
_____ Using oral language
_____ Developing print awareness
_____ Developing vocabulary

Physical Development

_____ Developing body awareness
_____ Developing fine motor skills
_____ Improving fitness
_____ Developing gross motor skills
_____ Developing eye-hand coordination
_____ Practicing creative movement
_____ Demonstrating space awareness

Arts

_____ Using creativity
_____ Practicing creative movement and dance

Music
_____ Exploring duration (long or short)
_____ Exploring pitch (high or low)
_____ Understanding form (AB—ABA)
_____ Exploring rhythm (beat or pulse)
_____ Keeping a steady beat
_____ Experimenting with tempo (speed—fast or slow)
_____ Experimenting with timbre and tone quality
_____ Exploring volume and dynamics

Visual Arts
_____ Working with lines
_____ Exploring shapes
_____ Understanding space
_____ Experimenting with color
_____ Using different textures

Social Interaction
_____ Engaging in cooperative play
_____ Demonstrating cultural appreciation and understanding
_____ Engaging in dramatic play
_____ Recognizing emotions
_____ Building self-confidence
_____ Sharing
_____ Developing social-emotional skills
_____ Practicing teamwork

Social Studies
_____ Learning about self, family, and community
_____ Learning about people and the environment
_____ Learning about history and events

Supporting Independent Learning

Next, consider how to support children who will be working more independently in learning centers as opposed to in whole group activities. Think about how you can adapt learning activities in ways that allow children to be more independent in the learning center. Consider the following ideas to help you provide support for children's autonomy:

- Providing picture cards with some words can help children to understand what to do at a learning center.

- Reviewing directions prior to releasing them to centers will help them to know options.

- Select portions of the lessons to complete in a whole group format prior to releasing children to centers.

- Interacting with children at learning centers to facilitate some learning activities.

- Inviting parents or other community volunteers to interact with children at a particular learning center.

Preparing for a New Learning Theme

Once you have established lessons and activities that coincide with different content areas, begin to review the ideas to see if any areas are missing or could be further enhanced. List and gather materials for use with specific themes, learning centers, and topics. Create picture cards or notes that will allow children to complete the activity independently in the learning center if needed. As the children play, you can observe and make adjustments to enhance skill development across learning centers and content areas. Enjoy using learning-center themes to promote children's growth and development in all areas.

Index